SECRET
TUCSON

A GUIDE TO THE WEIRD, WONDERFUL, AND OBSCURE

Clark Norton

Library of Congress Control Number: 2019936717

ISBN: 9781681062273

Design by Jill Halpin

Printed in the United States of America
22 23 24   5 4 3

To Catharine,
who has been with me for every step of the journey.

CONTENTS

ACKNOWLEDGMENTS

For their valuable assistance while researching this book, the author would like to thank Dan Gibson, James Martin, Al Young, Mitch Stevens, David Hoffman, Carina Garcia, Tom Skinner, Monica Cook, Daniel Reese, Stephen Hall, Richard Ratkevich, Peggy Feinman, Grace Gordon, Philip Block, Will Williams, Sheldon Clark, Veronica Daly, Scott Jacobs, Tom and Chris Sonnemann, Michael and Mary Reiter, Tom Philabaum, Mary Beth Norton, and to everyone else who offered suggestions for ideas. Special thanks go to Josh Stevens, Barbara Northcott, and Don Korte at Reedy Press for giving me the opportunity to write *Secret Tucson*; and to Grael Norton, Nona Patrick, Lia Norton, Michael Livermore, and Conrad Norton for their assistance and encouragement throughout. Finally, extra special thanks go to my wife, Catharine, who truly made this project possible.

INTRODUCTION

"Tucson is the weird capital of the world."
—Jodie Foster, in the 1974 film *Alice Doesn't Live Here Anymore*

Whether or not Tucson is—or ever was—the weird capital of the world, Tucsonans don't seem to shy away from the designation. Even Visit Tucson, the city's visitors bureau, posted the quote on its Facebook page. You might consider a shop that displays various ancient human skulls and some gold-leaf-covered mummified pack rats to be weird; many Tucsonans take it in stride. Or maybe you think it's a little weird to build a nice bar in a former mortuary; Tucson has two of them. Or that busy North Fourth Avenue has a twenty-five-ton tiki head staring out over it; makes perfect sense.

Or maybe it means Jodie Foster was right all along—and as a Tucsonan, you just get used to it.

Of course, those who know Tucson also know there are plenty of wonderful things here too: a white cactus flower that blankets the desert only one night a year, a children's fairyland park that was the life's work of a man who actually believed in fairies, a museum filled with kinetic sculptures made entirely from discarded junk. (Well, the weird and the wonderful might just overlap a bit.)

And then there is the obscure. Did you know that the westernmost battle of the Civil War was fought near Tucson? That Tucson actively promoted itself to tuberculosis sufferers as "the health seekers' mecca" in the early twentieth century? And that a famous New York crime boss lived out his last decades in (relative) quietude here? If so, you're ahead of where I was when I started researching this book.

So saddle up, settle in, and enjoy all the weird, the wonderful, and the obscure that is *Secret Tucson*.

—Clark Norton

1 GEMS, MINERALS, AND SO MUCH MORE

Where can you find a Roman gladiator's skull and mummified pack rats?

Yes, Tucson is famous for its huge two-week Gem, Mineral, and Fossil Showcase each February, but that still leaves fifty weeks of the year when Tucson Mineral and Gem World stands out. A family-owned business since the 1960s—the founder's two sons, Richard and Ron Ratkevich, now run it—the funky but friendly shop is situated amid saguaro-cacti-studded hillsides a few miles outside town.

The weathered wooden storefront is hard to miss—just look for the teepee and the fierce-looking T-Rex out front. Chances are you'll soon strike up a conversation with one of the owners, who will gladly point out some of the store's more unusual items. There are the gold-leaf-plated mummified pack rats, the ancient Mayan penis piercers (for ritual bloodletting), and, the pride of the collection, the human skulls. Secured within a glass case near the front of the shop, the skulls are said to have belonged to a Roman gladiator, an English witch, a Spanish conquistador,

TUCSON MINERAL AND GEM WORLD

WHAT Funky shop for gems and oddities

WHERE 801 S. Kinney Rd.

COST Free admission

PRO TIP They've probably got it. Just ask.

The store is en route to two of Tucson's most popular attractions, the outstanding Arizona-Sonora Desert Museum and Old Tucson, the Old West movie studio and theme park.

It's hard to miss Tucson Mineral and Gem World as you drive along S. Kinney Road—just look for the weathered wooden storefront and the fierce-looking T-Rex greeting you in the parking area.

a pirate, an Aztec sacrificial victim, and other long-deceased individuals, most of whom seem to have met an untimely demise.

The shelves and cabinets are packed with tens of thousands of gemstones, crystals, minerals, fossils, and artifacts, large and small, from around the world: tanzanite, malachite, selenite (a crystal big in metaphysical circles), garnets, quartz, agate bookends, meteorites, dinosaur bone and starfish fossils, Indian arrowheads, iron pyrite (fool's gold), ancient Egyptian artifacts, alabaster Buddhas, Neolithic pottery, Arizona souvenir rocks, turquoise jewelry, and fossil art made from four-hundred-million-year-old North African obsidian—and that's just for starters. Everything's for sale except the human skulls, just in case you were in the market for such—but don't let that keep you away. Can they interest you in a gold-plated pack rat?

² NO PASSWORD, NO PROBLEM

Pssst . . . Do you know where I can find a nice speakeasy?

You don't need a secret password, and it's not concealed behind a fake wall that swings open when you whisper "Frankie sent me." But the Tough Luck Club has a true speakeasy vibe to it, partly because you would never just stumble across it if you tried.

First you need to walk through Reilly, a very good Italian restaurant in downtown Tucson. Head toward the back (trying to ignore the wafting aromas of pastas and pizzas), hang a right, and enter Reilly's comfortable outdoor beer garden. Despite any pull you may feel to stop and relax with a brew there, fight it off and follow the single white arrow around a corner to a stairway that appears to go nowhere. But keep moving to a narrow basement bar where the atmosphere is cozy and classy but unpretentious. A long bar lines one wall and booths line another. It's seldom boisterous—but that may be because it occupies the space of a former mortuary. Welcome to the Tough Luck Club!

At the TLC, as devotees know it, you can get an expertly mixed, if pricey, craft cocktail (which can be as stiff as the prices, so take heed), or pay a few bucks for a shot of whiskey and a beer. The featured cocktails are creative and change out every four months. You can order off the menu or ask the bartender to surprise you. Whichever, you'll probably be pleasantly surprised by the result—as long as you can find your way down that staircase.

The Tough Luck Club, located in the basement of the Italian restaurant Reilly in downtown Tucson, occupies the space of a former mortuary and has a speakeasy vibe—partly because it's so well hidden.

TOUGH LUCK CLUB

WHAT A hidden bar with a speakeasy vibe

WHERE 101 E. Pennington St.

COST Drinks $4 to $14, less during happy hours

PRO TIP Happy hours are from 5 to 7 p.m. and midnight to 2 a.m.

A Prohibition-style Tucson speakeasy called the Still is even more secretive: you have to reserve in advance (Friday and Saturday nights only), then text 209-909-6299 to learn its location.

GOING BATTY

Why do waves of bridge bats appear at sunset?

Tucson's Mexican free-tail bats—yes, the flying mammals—are the opposite of the city's snowbirds. Unlike the humans who flock here to escape harsh northern winters, the bats migrate to Tucson in the heat of late spring and summer, then return to Mexico or Central America in the fall. There's method to their madness: Tucson's midsummer monsoon rains bring out the insects in droves, and bats feast on insects like kids inhale tater tots. According to the Arizona Game and Fish Department, hundreds of thousands of the furry flyers consume thousands of pounds of insects in Tucson each year, and that means fewer moths and mosquitoes to spoil your backyard barbecue.

Each April until October or so, and especially in peak monsoon season (July–September), the bats put on a show every evening at sunset, flying out by the thousands from underneath various Tucson bridges to lap up insects in their path. The bats roost under bridges because cracks and grooves offer them cozy spaces to squeeze in and enjoy sheltered sleep during the day. (It's said that five

BAT BRIDGE

WHAT Massive waves of bats

WHERE N. Campbell Ave. and River Rd.

COST Free

PRO TIP Arrive at least fifteen minutes before sunset so as not to miss the spectacle.

Bats are protected by law in Arizona and should not be disturbed, both for their good and yours—some bats carry rabies.

Waves of Mexican free-tail bats swoop out from under Tucson bridges each night at dusk during peak monsoon season (July to September), devouring tons of insects before flying back to their roosts as darkness falls.

hundred baby bats can hang out in one square foot beneath the bridges, and even a typical adult bat weighs only half an ounce.) Once darkness settles, the speedy bats zip back to their lairs and the spectacle is over.

Probably the most accessible bridge to watch this singular wildlife display, if you're so inclined, is the North Campbell Avenue Bridge over the Rillito River just south of River Road. Parking is available at various shops in the area, and you can watch from the top of the bridge. But intrepid souls who want to see the bats when they first emerge can watch from below the bridge—just beware of guano droppings. Wear hats—and bring the family!

BLOOMING AMAZING

What one-night-only horticultural event takes place in Tucson?

It's a once-in-a-year event: the mass blooming of the queen of the night (also known as night-blooming cereus), a type of cactus native to Arizona, New Mexico, west Texas, and northern Mexico. Sometime between late May and late July—for one night only—stunning white flowers open on the otherwise unremarkable stick-like cacti after sundown and then wilt and die by the following morning.

The vanilla-scented flowers can reach diameters of up to a foot, and since all the cacti in one area bloom on the same night, they create a spectacular array of white blossoms blanketing the desert. They are particularly notable in the Sonoran desert around Tucson, and the best, most convenient place to view them is at the Tohono Chul gardens on the northern fringes of the city. The forty-five-acre park boasts the largest collection of queen of the night cacti in the country.

As Tucson's intense summer heat develops, botanists at Tohono Chul keep close watch on signs indicating when the flowers will emerge. The park then stays open until late that evening for public viewing. As the local newspaper the *Arizona Daily Star* recently headlined, "Stop What You're Doing! Queen of the Night Is Blooming Tonight," adding that "you have to experience [it] at least once in your life."

Keeping in mind that there may be as little as twelve hours' notice of the event, you can sign up for email alerts at Tohono Chul's website (tohonochulpark.org).

On just one night each year, the queen of the night cactus blooms to reveal stunning white flowers blanketing the Sonoran desert; the best place to view this natural spectacle in Tucson is at the Tohono Chul gardens.

QUEEN OF THE NIGHT BLOOMING

WHAT A once-a-year chance to witness a blossoming cactus

WHERE 7366 N. Paseo del Norte

COST $5 (for this event)

PRO TIP Bring a flashlight and wear closed-toe walking shoes.

SIGNS OF LIFE

Where can I relive Tucson's neon past?

Opened in 2018, Ignite Sign Art Museum is both a product of one man's passions and an homage to Tucson's legacy of neon signage: a popular art form that reached its apex here from the late 1940s through the 1960s. Motels, diners, and other businesses competed to attract both locals and travelers with neon displays that are now considered classics of their type.

Jude Cook, who runs the museum along with his wife, Monica, is the Tucsonan most responsible for keeping that legacy alive into the twenty-first century. Cook has built or restored many of the most notable signs still visible around the city, including the iconic thirty-foot-high neon *Gateway Saguaro* on North Oracle Road, the old Pueblo Hotel diving girl at 145 South Sixth Avenue (now a spa), and the Tropicana Motor Hotel sign relocated from Miracle Mile to West Drachman Street.

The Cooks now showcase more than 350 other items in their sprawling indoor-outdoor museum space, which encompasses several rooms and totals some seven thousand square feet. It represents Jude Cook's personal collection spanning more than forty years and includes electric and hand-lettered advertising signs along with neon. One section is a tribute to signs of Tucson days gone by: the De Anza Drive-In movie theater, Jerry's Lee Ho Market,

IGNITE SIGN ART MUSEUM

WHAT A colorful collection of neon and historic signs

WHERE 331 S. Olsen Ave.

COST $12; seniors and military, $10; students and ages 6–17, $8

PRO TIP The museum space has café tables and is available for special events.

10

The new Ignite Sign Art Museum displays hundreds of original signs and replicas collected by Jude Cook, who has built or restored many of the most notable neon signs that add color and character to Tucson.

Magic Carpet Golf, and many more that long-time Tucsonans will recognize. A huge 76 gas station ball serves as a centerpiece; an illuminated KFC bucket is another eye-catcher. Most displays are from Tucson, but Cook's colorful collection includes signs from around Arizona and other states.

Don't miss the rear outdoor space, where you may be able to view some of Cook's sign restoration work in progress.

⁶ A SURPRISING SKIRMISH

Where was the westernmost Civil War battle fought?

Distinctively shaped Picacho Peak is a familiar sight to anyone driving between Tucson and Phoenix on Interstate 10. Located about forty-five miles northwest of Tucson and resembling a giant Spanish saddle, the 1,500-foot-high peak forms the centerpiece of Picacho Peak State Park, where you can hike, camp, and picnic.

What's far less known about Picacho Peak is that it was also the site of the westernmost battle of the Civil War—and the largest Arizona skirmish of that war—which took place on April 15, 1862. Two patrol parties, one Union, one Confederate, met that day at Picacho Pass, where they clashed in the shadow of the mountain and added an interesting footnote to the history of the war. The Union triumphed, though both sides suffered casualties. Every spring at the state park, history unfolds anew when volunteers stage a reenactment of the battle.

The Confederacy had briefly established a foothold in Tucson itself for two months between late February and late April of 1862, when more than one hundred Texas Rebels overran the then-small town's defenses at the Tucson Presidio and planted the Stars and Bars there. For a short time, Tucson became the Confederate capital of the Arizona Territory. But following the defeat of the Confederates at Picacho Pass, some 1,800 Union soldiers from California took back the Presidio with no shots fired.

BATTLE OF PICACHO PASS

WHAT The westernmost Civil War battle

WHERE Exit 219 off Interstate 10, Picacho

COST State park fee: $7 per vehicle for 4 persons; $3 per bicycle rider

PRO TIP Park trails are open sunrise to sunset year round.

Civil War reenactors dressed as Union soldiers re-create the Battle of Picacho Pass near Tucson, which proved to be the westernmost battle of the Civil War when Union and Confederate scouting parties clashed there.

Since the 1700s, six different flags have flown over Tucson: those of Spain, Mexico, the Confederate States of America, the Arizona Territory, the state of Arizona, and the United States.

HOLY MOAI!

What's that twenty-five-ton tiki head doing on Fourth Avenue?

When Magic Carpet Golf, a mini-golf course on East Speedway Boulevard in Tucson, closed down back in 2007, one of its most beloved features—a giant tiki head—was left homeless after forty years. But what do you do with a three-story-tall sculpture of an Easter Island head, known as a moai, and nicknamed Stone Face, that weighs fifty thousand pounds and spouts fire from the top of its head?

You find a tiki bar, of course, that's willing to host it, and then you figure out how to move it. The tiki bar—called the Hut, located on North Fourth Avenue, fulfilled the first obligation. Then came the hard part. A local group called "Save the Tiki" went about the task of fundraising for the operation, collecting $20,000 from Magic Carpet Golf fans, tiki devotees, and others who didn't want to see Stone Face reduced to rubble. Then, according to a newspaper report, a local artist, Tom Prevatt, agreed to renovate the head. The rest of the work was a team effort by Galileo Construction, Division 2 Construction, Broderick Engineers, Parson Steel Erectors, Caid Industries, Lanning Architects, and the Hut. The entire project took a year and a half, from 2008 to 2009.

When the relocation was complete, the Hut threw a block party to dedicate its new addition, which drew 1,500 people and featured several bands. Stone Face, originally built in 1969–1970, now stands tall over North Fourth—and while he never cracks a smile, he's got to be happy with the result.

TWENTY-FIVE-TON TIKI HEAD

WHAT A giant Easter Island-style statue

WHERE 305 N. 4th Ave.

COST Free

PRO TIP Head into the Hut if you crave Polynesian drinks and ambiance.

This twenty-five-ton, three-story-high tiki head, modeled after the moai heads of Easter Island, towers over Tucson's busy Fourth Avenue shopping district in front of a tiki bar, but it began life at a miniature golf course.

Nearby at 238 North Fourth Avenue, the Boxyard, which opened in 2019, is an outdoor food court and bar where the restaurants operate out of repurposed shipping containers.

⁸BEAR DOWN!

Where is UA sports icon "Button" Salmon buried?

While driving from Phoenix to Tucson in October 1926, John Byrd "Button" Salmon—star athlete and student body president at the University of Arizona—was critically injured in a car crash, leaving him paralyzed. With his quarterback near death two weeks later, football coach J. F. "Pop" McKale asked Salmon if he could relay any messages to his teammates. "Tell them . . . tell the team to bear down!" Salmon replied.

Salmon died the following day, four days before his twenty-third birthday, and McKale used his star's last words to inspire the team. The Wildcats went on to defeat New Mexico State 7–0 that week, and "Bear down" has served as UA sports teams' rallying cry for nearly a century since. The university's fight song, written in 1952, is called "Bear Down, Arizona." The motto was inscribed atop the campus gymnasium (called Bear Down Gym), and the university has even adopted the slogan "Bigger Questions. Better Answers. Bear Down." Salmon is memorialized on campus with a bronze bust near the Lowell-Stevens Football Facility, and UA's football team members now touch the bust during the "Wildcat Walk" before every home game.

Salmon's funeral attracted thousands of mourners, and he was laid to rest in Tucson's Evergreen Memorial Park, where plot number 22512267 is marked with a simple gravestone with his name and the dates "22 October 1903–18 October 1926," along with the inscription "Bear Down."

"Pop" McKale was himself a legend, coaching several major sports and serving as UA athletic director for forty-three years; UA's basketball arena, McKale Center, is named for him.

Most University of Arizona Wildcat fans know the school slogan "Bear Down!" but not everyone knows the tragic backstory of John Byrd "Button" Salmon, the football hero who coined that phrase, or where in Tucson he is buried.

JOHN BYRD SALMON GRAVE

WHAT Burial Site of "Bear Down" Icon

WHERE 3015 N. Oracle Rd.

COST Free

PRO TIP Check in at the Evergreen cemetery office for directions to the gravesite.

⁹ THE LOST TREASURE OF THE CATALINAS

Is a wealth of Spanish gold hidden in the mountains?

According to legend dating from the 1700s, a fabulously rich gold mine once known to early Spanish settlers lies hidden behind the Santa Catalina Mountains just north of Tucson, within the Cañada del Oro, or "pathway of gold." The mythical mine—variously known as the Lost Escalante Mine and the Iron Door Mine—has tantalized prospectors for centuries and made Tucson a must-stop on treasure hunters' itineraries.

The legend is associated with the story of Father Eusebio Francisco Kino, a Jesuit priest who established a mission in the late 1690s along the Santa Cruz River near modern-day Tucson. The Jesuits, assisted by the Spanish military—including a Captain Escalante—enslaved the local natives, forcing them to mine gold in the region. (The "Escalante" name may also derive from one of Kino's fellow priests who collected the gold.) When Spain expelled the Jesuits from America in 1767 for failing to pay their share of gold to the

THE LOST ESCALANTE MINE

WHAT Legendary lost gold mine

WHERE Somewhere in the Santa Catalinas (or not)

COST Free (and possibly profitable)

PRO TIP Good luck!

In 1880, two miners claimed they had found the Lost Escalante Mine and displayed one hundred pounds of gold nuggets to prove it, one of several reports involving different prospectors and locations.

According to legend, a fabulously rich gold mine sealed with an iron door by early Spanish missionaries is lost somewhere in or near the Catalina Mountains, putting Tucson on the treasure hunters' map.

Spanish crown, they were said to have sealed one particularly rich mine with an iron door—leaving a wealth of gold bullion secreted within.

Cynics have pointed out that some aspects of the legend, such as the sealed iron door itself, are suspiciously similar to those of other lost Spanish mine legends. But true believers contend a fortune in gold is there for the taking—and who's to say they're wrong?

AN ENCHANTED FANTASYLAND

Where can kids go to see a place where fairies live?

A believer in spiritualism, ghosts, fairies, the virtues of kindness, and the essential goodness of young children, Tucsonan George Phar Legler set about creating an enchanted land for families nearly a century ago. Legler's whimsical vision inspired the transformation of two acres in the northern part of the city into a delightful, non-commercial little theme park replete with stone sculptures, winding paths, secreted grottoes, and magic towers. With the help of friends—as well as two hundred tons of stone and eight hundred sacks of cement—Legler completed the project in 1932 after nearly a decade of work. He called his fantasyland the Valley of the Moon.

The park welcomed visitors from around the region and, as word of its charms spread, from the rest of the world as well. Legler staged frequent Bunnyland Theater shows, starring Jack, the rabbit; led Fairy Tours under his guise as the Mountain Gnome; made himself "disappear" into the Wizard's Tower; and guided children through the Enchanted Garden, where they might meet the Fairy Princess (played by his granddaughter). He used special effects to enhance the magical atmosphere and entrance all who entered.

But long plagued by ill health, Legler was forced to cut back his involvement, and by the 1960s the Valley of the Moon had

---

Legler was a member of the Fairy Investigation Society, an organization whose motto was "We welcome all who have the Fairy Faith." Another member: Walt Disney.

The gateway to the Valley of the Moon leads to a children's fairyland, which an eccentric Tucsonan—who himself believed in fairies, ghosts, and spiritualism—built and made his life's work.

fallen into disrepair. Legler, who died in 1982 at the age of ninety-seven, handed over operations to a group of dedicated volunteers, and it is run today by a nonprofit society. While the park is now open only sporadically, it remains an only-in-Tucson place that continues to entertain and enchant the children to whom the Mountain Gnome devoted his life.

VALLEY OF THE MOON

WHAT A fantasyland for young children

WHERE 2544 E. Allen Rd.

COST Free first Saturday of each month; $5 on third Sunday for history tours; private tours $10 by reservation (520-323-1331)

PRO TIP Open the first Saturday of each month "around sundown."

11 SONGS OF LOVE AND SADNESS

Why do top mariachi bands gather here each year?

They're familiar figures in many Mexican restaurants and fiestas: strolling mariachis resplendent in their traditional traje de charro outfits—embroidered short-cut jackets with white or gold trim, pants ornamented with silver or gold plating, wide-brimmed sombreros, and floppy ties. They strum guitars, play violins and trumpets, and serenade their audiences with songs about love and sadness. It's a Mexican folkloric tradition that began in the countryside in the nineteenth century and has since been adopted by the entire country for entertaining at weddings and other celebrations, Catholic masses, and even funerals.

While mariachi music has deep roots in Mexico, Tucson has been the most influential American city in promoting its popularity across the United States, and mariachi music has come to symbolize the city's strong cross-border culture. The

TUCSON INTERNATIONAL MARIACHI CONFERENCE

WHAT A showcase for mariachi music

WHERE 5655 W. Valencia Rd.

COST Concert $43–$300

PRO TIP Ticket proceeds benefit La Frontera children's services.

When Guadalajara, Mexico, where mariachi music was born, decided to hold its own mariachi conference, representatives traveled to Tucson to study how to do it right.

Mariachi music originated in Mexico, but Tucson has played a major role in popularizing it throughout the United States. The annual Tucson International Mariachi Conference hosts top acts and workshops.

annual Tucson International Mariachi Conference, held here for several days each April since 1982, is one big reason why. The conference brings together some of the world's top mariachi bands and dancers to perform, to teach, and to keep this heritage alive. (Tucson native Linda Ronstadt, a one-time rock star who also sang mariachi, played an early role in its success.)

Most recently, the conference has been held in the Grand Ballroom at Tucson's Casino del Sol. The lineup includes workshops for students and vocal competitions for children. At the closing "Espectacular Concert," top bands blast the harmonies of stringed and brass instruments from the stage, while folkloric dancers add vibrant swirls of color to the performances.

BILL CLINTON'S FABULOUS FEAST

Where can you chow down like a (former) president?

When former President Bill Clinton visited Mi Nidito, a longtime Mexican restaurant in South Tucson, he brought along his famously prodigious, pre-vegan appetite. The date was February 25, 1999. According to an account the next day in the *Arizona Daily Star*, Clinton just kept ordering course after course: "First, waitress Virginia Lopez brought a chile relleno. Then the president downed a chicken enchilada. He moved on to a bean tostada, then took up two more courses: a shredded beef taco with a flour tortilla and a beef tamale. All that and rice and beans, too." (And for the record, portions are large there anyway.)

As you might expect, Mi Nidito, Spanish for "my little nest," has capitalized on the notoriety ever since, drawing lines of hungry diners to its doors for years. And, not to let any marketing opportunity pass by, the restaurant offers what's now known as the "President's Plate": a quintuple whammy combo of the Clinton signature order, all served with rice and beans, for $15.95. It's become a popular—and completely bipartisan—menu item.

As for Clinton, the *Daily Star* reported that he later confessed to one of his eight dining companions (mostly local politicos): "I ate too much."

MI NIDITO RESTAURANT

WHAT Site of the ex-president's feast

WHERE 1813 S. 4th Ave., South Tucson

COST $15.95; (smaller) combo plates $9.50 and up

PRO TIP Tables usually fill up by 5 p.m. or earlier on weekends.

Tucson's Mi Nidito Mexican restaurant earned its place on the culinary map when then-President Bill Clinton stopped by for lunch and proceeded to devour five big courses including tortillas, rice, and beans; it now offers the "President's Plate" for those who dare to tackle it.

Other famous Mi Nidito guests have included Madeleine Albright, Enrique Iglesias, Willie Nelson, Linda Ronstadt, Rich Little, William Shatner, Kurt Russell, Beau Bridges, Sam Elliot, Sean Elliot, and Steve Kerr.

¹³ MIRROR IMAGES

What cutting-edge scientific laboratory is located beneath a football stadium?

First, you have to find it. The instructions sound like something out of a spy novel:

"We are located on the east side of UA Football Stadium. Please look for Gate 4 of the football stadium, follow the sidewalk south to the Mirror Lab entrance. Look for two blue benches." You're tempted to add: "Then leave the package on the second bench. Make sure you haven't been followed. Walk slowly away from the stadium . . ."

But no, these are the instructions for finding the Richard F. Caris Mirror Lab, surely the only notable scientific lab in the country located under a football stadium (in this case that of the University of Arizona). Within that space, a team of scientists and engineers are making the largest and most advanced spun-cast telescope mirrors in the world—enabling the production of giant optical telescopes that will explore the deepest realms of outer space.

During ninety-minute tours of the facility, visitors hear that the key to the mirrors' power is a honeycomb structure, an innovation that makes them far superior to the solid-glass mirrors used in past conventional telescopes. While they retain the rigidity and stability of the older telescopes, the honeycomb mirrors enable new telescopes to be much larger, lighter, and more powerful.

The lab is developing the mirrors for the super-powerful Giant Magellan Telescope now being constructed in Las Campanas, Chile, expected to be operational by 2025.

Doubtless the only cutting-edge scientific facility in the country located beneath a football stadium, the Richard F. Caris Mirror Lab builds mirrors for super-powered telescopes, including the Giant Magellan Telescope, pictured here.

RICHARD F. CARIS MIRROR LAB

WHAT Cutting-edge telescope work

WHERE 527 National Championship Dr.

COST $20

PRO TIP Tours are offered afternoons Monday through Friday.

The new technology had an unlikely beginning. Back in 1980, Dr. Roger Angel, the lab's founder and scientific director, tried a backyard experiment: fusing together two custard cups in an improvised kiln to test the suitability of borosilicate glass for making honeycomb structures. It worked, and five years later, the Mirror Lab was born. Using a series of increasingly larger rotating furnaces, the lab has produced ever larger mirrors, now up to twenty-seven and a half feet wide. And it's all happening under a football stadium.

<u>14</u> TOY TRAIN LOVERS' DREAM

Where can you see some of Tucson's top model railways?

Engines chug along tiny tracks. Whistles blow, alerting the little farms and villages ahead that mini-trains are about to emerge from mountain tunnels or tree-lined valleys just beyond the bend. Look carefully and you'll spot a Mexican village, complete with cantina, bodega, and a mission church. Down the way are pocket-sized towns with vintage diners and motels.

Round and round they go, these model freight and passenger trains (and occasional trolleys and monorails) of the Gadsden-Pacific Division Toy Train Operating Museum, eliciting squeals of delight from youngsters and captivating adults as well. Besides evoking the romance, nostalgia, and intricate designs and mechanics of train travel, they're just plain fun to watch amid the riot of sights, sounds, and beautifully crafted layouts. Some displays are interactive—push a button and lights flash! And don't forget to look up: some trains run overhead.

Situated in a northwest Tucson warehouse that's well off the beaten track, so to speak, the museum is staffed by volunteers, many of them retirees and other dedicated hobbyists, on hand to answer questions and share their love of "toy" trains. Open to the public just twice a month from fall to spring, as

The separate Tucson Garden Railway Society runs free, self-guided "Rails in the Garden Tours" one weekend each winter, visiting elaborate outdoor model train layouts at private residences (tucsongrs.org).

Model railways chug along tiny tracks at Tucson's Gadsden-Pacific Division Toy Train Operating Museum, charming children and adults alike as the trains blow their whistles and glide through beautifully crafted layouts.

GADSDEN-PACIFIC DIVISION TOY TRAIN OPERATING MUSEUM

WHAT A place to enjoy model trains

WHERE 3975 N. Miller Ave.

COST Free

PRO TIP Open second and fourth Sundays of the month, 12:30 to 4:30 p.m.; closed summers.

well as for birthday parties, kids' workshops, and other special events, the museum relies on donations and mostly word-of-mouth publicity.

The six inside layouts are continually changing, each featuring a different "scale," or track and train size, ranging from the largest (G scale) to the smallest (N scale). And outside, there's a 7.5-inch gauge riding train that carries passengers around the building when operational. A real train car, Rio Grande Caboose #01433, also stands outside and is available to tour.

15 HOBNOBBING WITH THE SNOBS

Where did the affluent Tucson elite build their grand mansions?

After the arrival of the Southern Pacific Railroad in the 1880s, Tucson attracted wealthy Easterners who didn't fancy inhabiting the Sonoran row houses then predominant in town. Adobe was out, imported building materials and new architectural styles were in. Along North Main Avenue in the historic El Presidio Neighborhood, where Tucson was born, the railroad and copper barons and affluent locals lived in grand mansions where they threw equally grand parties, formed private clubs, and, reportedly, lorded it over the locals. The same locals soon dubbed the area "Snob Hollow."

Though possibly snobbish, the wealthy elite weren't entirely impractical. Several dwellings were converted adobes renovated to resemble styles then in vogue on the East and West Coasts. One example is the Sam Hughes house at 221 North Main, built in 1865 and expanded into a Greek Revival gem. (Hughes, who had made his fortune in Tucson, needed the extra room for his ten children.) Another is the Julius Kruttschnitt house at 297 North Main, which originally dated from 1876 and was redone with Victorian flourishes (it's now a stylish B&B, the El Presidio Inn).

Others were built entirely post-1880 in Mission Revival style. The 1905 Cheyney House at 252 North Main was home

Sonoran adobes dressed up as Victorians, such as Snob Hollow's Julius Kruttschnitt house, became known in architectural circles as "American Territorial" style.

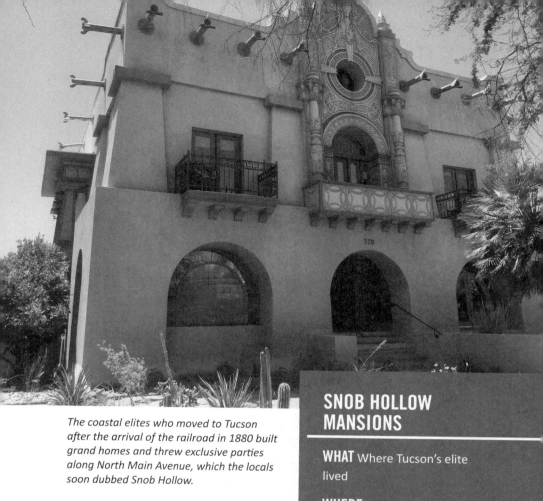

The coastal elites who moved to Tucson after the arrival of the railroad in 1880 built grand homes and threw exclusive parties along North Main Avenue, which the locals soon dubbed Snob Hollow.

SNOB HOLLOW MANSIONS

WHAT Where Tucson's elite lived

WHERE N. Main Ave. between W. Washington and W. Franklin Sts.

COST Free

PRO TIP While in the neighborhood, stop in to visit the Tucson Museum of Art, just down the block.

to the widow of a postmaster and survived a 1981 fire, after which it was completely restored. A second, the 1907 J. Knox Corbett house at 180 North Main, belonged to a future mayor. And the 1900s-era Steinfeld mansion at 300 North Main served briefly as Tucson's original Owls Club, founded by thirteen eligible Snob Hollow bachelors. It was restored in 1985 after falling into disrepair, as did several of the homes along North Main. Today, the tree-lined street is once again an architectural showplace—sans snobbishness, of course.

16 RECYCLING FOR PARENTS

What can you do with your kids' outgrown stuff?

Little Bird Nesting Company, whose slogan is "Tucson's Cutest Resale Boutique," is a godsend to budget-minded new parents. As parents of young children know, they tend to grow out of their clothing quite quickly—and sometimes never even get to wear that cute little outfit that was a gift or an impulse purchase. Similarly, baby gear such as strollers, highchairs, booster seats, cribs, and the like get outgrown, as do toys and games.

This is where Little Bird comes to the rescue. You can bring your new or "gently used" items into the store for evaluation, and if they meet the store's standards, Little Bird will offer cash or trade for the items, which are suitable for babies, toddlers, and kids up to age eight. Depending on the age, condition, and current popularity of the item, the store offers anywhere from 40 to 70 percent of the retail price in trade (redeemable for anything in the store) or from 25 to 50 percent of the retail price in cash. Items must be clean and, in the case of gear, include all the original parts and be in working condition.

The store also keeps prices low so that parents can trade in one stroller, for instance, and leave with another more suitable one for a final cost well below that of most other

Unless you've brought in too many items to evaluate right then, the transactions are completed on the spot—and you never have to wait for consignment sales.

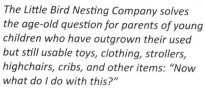

The Little Bird Nesting Company solves the age-old question for parents of young children who have outgrown their used but still usable toys, clothing, strollers, highchairs, cribs, and other items: "Now what do I do with this?"

LITTLE BIRD NESTING COMPANY

WHAT A store for "recycling" kids' clothes and toys

WHERE 4508 E. Broadway Blvd.

COST Free (to browse)

PRO TIP No appointment needed—just bring your items in.

stores. And there's the added benefit of cleaning out your closets by "recycling" outgrown or unwanted clothing, gear, and toys. Of course, if you're just shopping and not trading anything in, Little Bird still offers some of the best deals for kid stuff in Tucson—something just about every parent can appreciate.

THAT'S NO MIRAGE

Where can I cast a line in Tucson?

It used to be that when you hung up a "Gone fishing" sign in Tucson, it implied you'd be gone for at least the better part of a day, heading off to one of southern Arizona's natural lakes. That was before the Arizona Game & Fish Department's Urban Fishing Program started back in 1985. Of twenty-one urban lakes that have been designated for fishing around the state, three are within Tucson's city limits, and the other is in nearby Sahuarita.

Of the three in Tucson, Kennedy Lake is the most "hidden"— difficult to find if you don't know exactly where to look for

it. In fact, even upon entering southwest Tucson's John F. Kennedy Park, where the lake is located, it's not obvious there's any body of water there at all. Nor is the signage very helpful.

But once you come upon the ten-acre reservoir, you can actually feel the breezes pick up as they carry onto the small beach area dotted with picnic tables and ramadas. Fishing,

KENNEDY LAKE

WHAT A place to fish in the city

WHERE 3600 S. La Cholla Blvd.

COST Free, with $24 annual fishing license

PRO TIP The best times to fish are early morning and evening.

though, is the main activity, and families casting lines are much in evidence. The lake is seasonally stocked from September to June with catfish, largemouth bass, sunfish, and rainbow trout. There are daily limits—four catfish, four trout, two bass, ten sunfish—and if you're over age ten you must have a special urban fishing license or risk a small fine. Some other rules and regulations also apply: no feeding the ducks and geese, no swimming or wading, and no boats with gasoline motors (canoes and licensed small boats are okay).

Kennedy Lake is a popular urban fishing spot, for those who can find it. The ten-acre reservoir is seasonally stocked with catfish, bass, sunfish, and trout.

Tucson's other urban lakes that allow fishing are Silverbell Lake at Christopher Columbus Park on North Silverbell Road and Lakeside Lake at Lakeside Park on East Stella Road.

ARIZONA'S FIRST COMMERCIAL VINEYARD

What does southern Arizona have in common with Burgundy, France?

While only an hour's drive southeast of Tucson, the little town of Sonoita seems much farther away. At an elevation of five thousand feet, it's typically cooler than the city, with summertime temperatures often in the eighties, and its landscape is mainly high-desert rolling grasslands dotted with ash and oak trees (no cacti).

It's also home to the region with the largest concentration of wineries and vineyards in Arizona, known as the Sonoita Wine Country. The composition of the red clay soil there has been likened to that of Burgundy. And even the arid climate is favorable in some regards—helping to fend off certain pests and reducing the need for pesticides—while rot, mold, and mildew are rare.

SONOITA VINEYARDS

WHAT Arizona's first commercial vineyard

WHERE 290 Elgin Canelo Rd., Sonoita

COST Tasting $10 (five wines, includes souvenir glass)

PRO TIP Tastings are much less crowded on weekdays.

Sonoita Vineyards, which opened in 1983, is the oldest commercial vineyard and winery in the state and has grown to include some thirty acres of hillside vines; its first plantings date back to 1979. (The founder, Dr. Gordon Dutt, was a soil scientist at the University of Arizona.) Most of its wines are made from grapes harvested on the estate, and all of its grapes come from southeastern Arizona.

Opened in 1983, Sonoita Vineyard is Arizona's oldest commercial winery and flagship of the Sonoita Wine Country near Tucson, whose soil has been likened to that of Burgundy, France. You can sample Sonoita's wines in their tasting room.

Bottlings are done by hand and kept to a small scale, in batches of less than two thousand per vintage, totaling four to five thousand cases a year. Wines range from sauvignon blanc to cabaret sauvignon and also include chardonnay, merlot, pinot noir, and syrah. The winery's tasting counter can hold twelve to twenty people, and in harvest season from late August to early September you can watch the wines being produced.

Ken's Shuttle Service (520-604-6939) offers safe and sober transportation along the Sonoita Wine Country Trail, where there are a dozen vineyards and tasting rooms.

Why does the *Gateway Saguaro* read "Miracle Mile"?

Tucson is awash with public art—sculptures, murals, even bridges—but the *Gateway Saguaro* sculpture may be the most significant, if not entirely understood. First, it's thirty feet tall. Dominating the median toward the southern tip of North Oracle Road, it's a commanding presence, especially at night when it's neon lit, with light bulbs lining the sides of the top half.

The saguaro, of course, is the region's iconic cactus, so it's only appropriate that, while driving toward downtown, the word "Tucson" is emblazoned on the sculpture's north-facing side. But why, when coming from the opposite direction, does it read "Miracle Mile"? After all, the actual Miracle Mile roadway is a fair distance north of the sculpture itself and no longer serves as a main gateway into the city.

The local artist who created the project in 2010, Dirk Arnold, told the *Arizona Daily Star* at the time that "I designed it as a two-way gateway" and added, according to the *Star*, that "he was driven by nostalgia for the giant neon signs that used to line Miracle Mile but are now close to extinct."

The good news: some of the "extinct" have been restored and reborn nearby, a kind of Jurassic Park for vintage signs that once advertised now-defunct businesses. Turning down West Drachman Street, just south of the *Gateway Saguaro*,

---

Arnold's design was chosen over forty competitors and cost $67,000 to build, paid for by funds for removing the roundabout that had previously occupied the spot.

The 30-foot-high neon Gateway Saguaro has become a local icon since its creation in 2010, just as the saguaro cactus is an iconic symbol of Tucson itself. But why does one side of it read "Miracle Mile"?

you'll find that classics like Magic Carpet Golf, the Tropicana Motor Hotel, and the Canyon State Motor Lodge live on. Mounted on fifteen-foot poles, they light up the street behind Pima Community College's downtown campus.

GATEWAY SAGUARO

WHAT An iconic public sculpture

WHERE N. Oracle Rd. north of W. Drachman St.

COST Free

PRO TIP North Oracle Road becomes North Main Avenue just after Drachman Street, which can be confusing.

JOHN DILLINGER'S BAD DAY

What led to the capture of the infamous bank robber?

For infamous bank robbers, John Dillinger and his armed gang sure knew how to mess up—they were done in by a series of happenstances in Tucson that made them look more like the Gang that Couldn't Shoot Straight. Dillinger and his cohorts were arrested here in January 1934, and many locals regard the event as one of the great moments in city law enforcement. But the really fascinating stuff is in the often-overlooked details.

Dillinger and three of his gang members, Harry Pierpont, Charles Makley, and Russell Clark, arrived in Tucson on January 21, 1934, and rented a house on North Second Avenue. But because the floors of the house had recently been waxed, they moved downtown to the Hotel Congress (blunder number one). Early on the morning of January 23, the hotel caught fire, and firemen, unknowingly, helped rescue the gang's weighty gun-laden luggage from their upper-floor rooms. Dillinger's crew gratefully tipped the firemen twelve dollars, a sizeable sum back then (blunder number two).

Suspicious of the gang's largesse and their heavy baggage, the firemen tipped off police. All four gang members were later captured—each arrested at different times and places on January 25. Dillinger's henchmen fell first: Makley was taken while running an errand, Clark was captured at the house

---

The Hotel Congress celebrates the anniversary of Dillinger's capture, complete with reenactments, during its annual Dillinger Days, the third weekend of January.

JOHN DILLINGER: PUBLIC ENEMY #1

The Dillinger gang and their lady friends registered under aliases at the Hotel Congress on the night of January 21, 1934. Early the next morning a fire broke out. The Tucson Fire Department used an aerial ladder to rescue the gang members from their third floor rooms. J. C. Davies, aka Charles Makley, tipped a fireman $12.00 to retrieve their luggage. The fireman noticed that the bags were unusually heavy (AHS# BN200435).

John Herbert Dillinger dominated headlines during the 1930s, when criminals were bold and the sounds of machine-gun fire and speeding getaway cars were common in many cities. He stole more money in twelve months than Jesse James had pilfered in sixteen years. Armed with machine guns, automatic rifles, and bulletproof vests, the Dillinger gang outgunned most police departments. Dillinger and gang members Harry Pierpont, Charles Makley, and Russell Clark were wanted in the Midwest for crimes ranging from murder to bank robbery when they arrived in Tucson, Arizona, with their lady friends Evelyn "Billie" Frechette, Mary Kinder, and Opal Long, to "lay low."

Notorious bank robber John Dillinger and his gang were arrested in Tucson in 1934 following a series of blunders that would make the Keystone Cops look good. Dillinger himself was collared at a house on a quiet residential street after the last of those blunders.

on North Second Avenue, and Pierpont actually drove himself to the police station, where he was arrested, having been tricked into going there by police (blunders three, four, and five).

Dillinger himself was captured later that day at the North Second Avenue house, unaware of Clark's earlier arrest there (blunder number six). He was then sent to jail in Indiana, where he soon escaped—only to be gunned down by federal agents in Chicago seven months later.

DILLINGER CAPTURE HOUSE

WHAT Dillinger was nabbed here

WHERE 927 N. Second Ave.

COST Free

PRO TIP This is a private residence, so do not disturb the occupants.

21

MONDAY MOVEMENT

Why do so many say "Meet me at Maynards"?

On a cold Colorado evening in December 2008, Tucsonan Jannie Cox was driving to dinner with her husband, Dave Syverson, when she noticed that hundreds of people of all ages and accoutrements (baby strollers, dogs) were running or briskly walking through downtown Colorado Springs. Intrigued, she soon learned that it was a regular weekly event sponsored by a local Irish pub—which, not coincidentally, did pretty good business after the run was over.

The two of them then wondered: why couldn't such an event be transplanted to Tucson, helping to stimulate both physical activity and downtown growth? Lining up the Southern Arizona Roadrunners as sponsors soon helped make the idea a reality. And thus was born Meet Me at Maynards, which has now been drawing eclectic crowds of walkers and runners to the city's center on Monday evenings for more than a decade.

After registering at Maynards Market & Kitchen, a top-notch restaurant in the city's historic railway complex, participants are given maps that cover a four-mile route through downtown and nearby areas, passing by restaurants and other interesting venues. Two- and three-mile-long options are provided for those who want a shorter workout. Registrants also receive hand stamps that entitle them to discounts at two

---

Restaurants offering discounts to registrants include Maynards, the Cup Café, Charro Steak, El Charro, Downtown Kitchen + Cocktails, Reilly Craft Pizza, Boca Tacos y Tequila, and Magpies Gourmet Pizza.

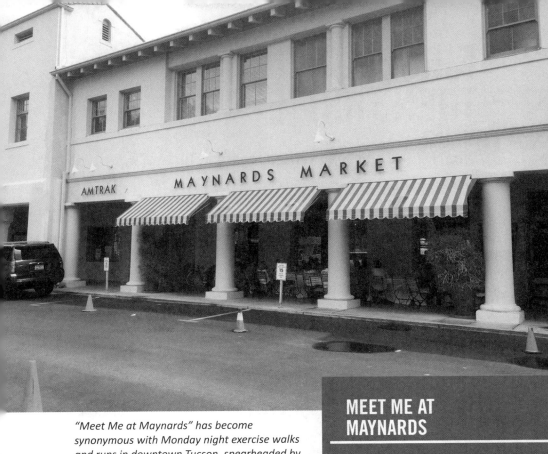

"Meet Me at Maynards" has become synonymous with Monday night exercise walks and runs in downtown Tucson, spearheaded by one local couple who took their inspiration from a chance sighting of a similar event in Colorado Springs, Colorado.

MEET ME AT MAYNARDS

WHAT A weekly walk or run

WHERE 400 N. Toole Ave.

COST Free

PRO TIP Meet at 5:15 p.m. on Monday nights, year-round.

dozen of those restaurants along the route, helping to spur business on what is traditionally a slow dining-out night.

And so, with perhaps unlikely origins on the wintry streets of Colorado Springs, Meet Me at Maynards has helped lead the revitalization of downtown Tucson—just one good reason to lace up those sneakers and get moving on Mondays.

22

FIRST SURVIVE, THEN THRIVE

What is the Chinese-American legacy in Tucson?

Chinese culture in Tucson began with the young men who labored to build the railroads that, by 1880, would provide Tucson with a comparatively fast, comfortable link to the rest of the United States. But life for the Chinese immigrants who came to Tucson in search of the promise of Gold Mountain (as America was known to them) was challenging. They faced culture shock, arduous working conditions, poverty, discrimination, opium addiction, and isolation in makeshift Chinatowns on the fringes of downtown Tucson.

Still, over the years, as families immigrated and were reunited, the growing Chinese community here launched small businesses—grocery stores, laundries, restaurants—and built schools and churches. Chinese associations that provided assistance in helping immigrants get footholds played a key role. As the old Chinatowns were razed by new housing developments and urban renewal projects, Chinese residents moved throughout Tucson, often to be near their

CHINESE CULTURAL CENTER

WHAT Tucson's Chinese-American heritage

WHERE 1288 W. River Rd.

COST Free

PRO TIP Tai chi and mahjongg are among classes offered at the center.

With a largely Hispanic clientele, many of the 1940s-era mom-and-pop grocers concocted hybrid items such as "Chinese chorizo."

A white lion marks the entrance to Tucson's impressive Chinese Cultural Center, where exhibits and activities reflect the remarkable success of the Chinese-American community in Tucson, which began with immigrants coming to work on the railroads in the late nineteenth century and who subsequently overcame decades of discrimination.

new ventures. They eventually became an integral part of the entire city fabric, and today Tucson and Pima County have about ten thousand Chinese-American residents.

A good place to learn about the history of Chinese-Americans in Tucson is the Chinese Cultural Center, a contemporary 15,600-square-foot building in the northern part of the city, that exemplifies the extraordinary success of their once-impoverished community here. Two white lions flank the entrance, while a twenty-seven-foot-high tower represents the bow of a symbolic ship as it came "ashore" carrying immigrants to the desert.

In the center's main hallway, which is open to the public, exhibits depict the mid-twentieth-century history of Tucson's many Chinese-owned "mom and pop" grocery stores, which were primarily located in heavily Hispanic districts; only a few survive. Prominent design elements, including circular moon gates, pay homage to Chinese architectural traditions.

23 A BRILLIANT BRIDGE

What will you see at 8:30 a.m. each March 20?

Tucson's Luis G. Gutierrez Bridge, completed in 2012, is the first four-pronged multi-use transportation link of its kind in Arizona. Cars, bicycles, streetcars, and pedestrians all rely on it to conveniently cross over the Santa Cruz River between downtown and parts of the city's west side. But only pedestrians can partake in a surprising interactive experience that those in vehicles cannot see—one that makes a stroll across the bridge a destination in itself.

That was the intent of local architect David Dobler, who designed the bridge to incorporate information about twelve historically significant local events displayed on its two sidewalks. These include facts about the annual rodeo parade, Father Eusebio Kino (who established the first mission here in the 1690s), the Southern Pacific Railroad (which opened up Tucson to the wider world), Mexican-style mariachi bands, the summer monsoon rains, and the Tucson Presidio (site of the first European settlement here), along with six more.

But Dobler took it a step further, designing shade canopies that hover over the sidewalks, with twelve icons cut into them that, at a specific time on a specific date each year, form images projected by the sun onto the sidewalks to illustrate each historical event. For instance, assuming the sun is shining, each March 20 at 8:30 a.m. you'd see a railway spike that marks the arrival of

---

LUIS G. GUTIERREZ BRIDGE

WHAT A surprise for pedestrians

WHERE W. Cushing St. between S. Linda Ave. and I-10

COST Free

PRO TIP Use the underpass to walk safely under the bridge to view both sidewalks.

Because of its creative design, the Luis G. Gutierrez Bridge over the Santa Cruz riverbed honors twelve significant events in Tucson's history by reflecting sunlit images on its pedestrian sidewalks at specific days and times during the year.

the railroad on that date in 1880. Each August 20 at 9:30 a.m. a mission bell appears, celebrating the founding of the Presidio in 1775. Each July 3 at 10:45 a.m. an image of a saguaro cactus marks the traditional start of monsoon season (and the annual harvesting of saguaro fruit by Native Americans). And each February 19 at 8:45 a.m. an airplane propeller marks Tucson's first airplane flight in 1910.

Other particularly interesting dates and times to watch for include June 1 at noon, commemorating Tucson's first electric streetcar, and Feb. 21 at 8:45 a.m., marking the city's first Rodeo Parade in 1925.

Why did Oscar winner Lee Marvin settle in Tucson?

Movie tough guy Lee Marvin, an ex-Marine who starred in such hits as *Cat Ballou* and *The Dirty Dozen* over the course of a prolific film and TV career that spanned from 1951 to 1986, abandoned California for a quieter life in Tucson in 1975. Moving to the desert as a means of avoiding the Hollywood spotlight, the Academy Award-winning actor was nonetheless active in the community and was frequently spotted at some of his favorite haunts—a diner, an Irish pub, a barber shop, a gun shop, a hardware store, even a blacksmith shop—near the home he and his wife, Pam, purchased in the Catalina foothills.

That home, built in 1936 and set on thirteen acres, had been designed by Tucson's then-best-known architect, the Swiss-born Josias Joesler. Along with stunning mountain views and a hillside of saguaros, the Spanish Mission-style house featured seven bathrooms, eight bedrooms, a game room, wrought-iron fixtures (forged by the blacksmith), beamed ceilings, a pool, a tennis court, a guest house, a courtyard with fountain, and lots of patio space. But the unpretentious Marvin liked to drive around in his battered 1971 pickup to avoid any starstruck fans. "They see you driving around in a pickup and that's it," he told a reporter. "They leave you alone."

While Marvin rode horses in many Western movies, including his Oscar-winning turn in *Cat Ballou*, he refused to saddle up after moving here "unless they offer me a lot of money."

LEE MARVIN HOUSE

WHAT Movie star's onetime home

WHERE 5353 N. Camino Escuela

COST Free

PRO TIP The private residence is on a dirt road near the intersection of N. Campbell Ave. and River Rd.

Hollywood tough guy and Academy Award-winning actor Lee Marvin moved to Tucson after shooting a film here and found the kind of laid-back community he had been looking for in the city's foothills. His Spanish-style house was designed by well-known architect Josias Joesler.

One of Marvin's first visits to Tucson came while filming the Western *Monte Walsh* at Old Tucson Studios in 1969. During the shoot, a drought had hit the region and threatened the cattle of the Tohono O'odham tribe with starvation; Marvin and co-star Jack Palance pitched in to load trucks with feed. Later, after moving to Tucson, Marvin was active in local wildlife conservation efforts. He died of a heart attack in Tucson in 1987 and is buried in Arlington National Cemetery.

25 AN UNLIKELY TRANSPLANT

What's a legendary Northern lumberjack doing in the desert?

A twenty-foot-tall fiberglass statue of Paul Bunyan—the legendary giant of a lumberjack said to have cleared vast forests and created entire bodies of water with his superhuman strength, his trusty axe, and his faithful companion Babe the Blue Ox—has amused Tucsonans since 1964. You really can't miss it as you pass by the intersection of North Stone Avenue and Glenn Street.

But why is a statue of this bearded folk hero, said to have hailed from the heavily forested Upper Midwest and to have labored as well in the cold and damp of the Pacific Northwest, baking down here in the desert sun? According to the Toia family, who have owned various businesses at that location since 1946—including their current one, Don's Hot Rod Shop—the late Leo Toia bought the statue in San Francisco and hauled it down to Tucson in a truck, where he installed it in the parking lot in front of his auto parts store as a kind of outsized business card. What better way to let your customers know how to find you?

Over the years, Bunyan has been decorated for Christmas, wearing a Santa costume and with giant candy canes replacing his axe, as well as holding an American flag during 1991's

The Paul Bunyan statue is one of a number of 1960s-era towering fiberglass "Muffler Men" figures designed to call attention to roadside businesses such as auto shops and diners.

A 20-foot-tall fiberglass statue of the legendary north woods lumberjack Paul Bunyan, complete with his trusty axe, has found a home in the desert sun in the parking lot of a Tucson auto parts shop.

PAUL BUNYAN STATUE

WHAT A towering lumberjack

WHERE N. Stone Ave. and Glenn St.

COST Free

PRO TIP For the best full view of Paul Bunyan, drive north on North Stone until you reach Glenn St.

Operation Desert Storm, and even as a member of ZZ Top wielding a guitar, which won a local radio station contest for creativity. The mighty lumberjack has also suffered the indignities of vandalism and attempted theft, but through it all has managed to stand tall, with the help of the occasional paint job to keep him fresh through those blistering Tucson summers.

ANCIENT AGRICULTURE

Where can you find crops grown four thousand years ago?

Archaeological evidence shows that Native Americans started growing crops in present-day Tucson more than four thousand years ago, making it the oldest continually cultivated place in America. That historic distinction is one reason why UNESCO named Tucson a "world capital of gastronomy" in 2015, the first city in the United States to be so honored.

Mission Garden, opened in 2012 and still a work in progress, is a four-acre compound that sits at the eastern foot of "A" Mountain (Sentinel Peak)—the place where prehistoric Tucson was born—and is a re-creation of the adobe-walled garden that supplied the Spanish Colonial-era San Agustín Mission. It's also an outdoor museum where you can walk through thousands of years of local agricultural history, starting with the wild corn, beans, squash, and cotton cultivated in 2100 BC. (Earlier occupants, dating from as long as twelve thousand years ago, relied on native edible cacti and medicinal plants to survive.)

MISSION GARDEN

WHAT Local crops through the ages

WHERE 946 W. Mission Ln.

COST $5 donation

PRO TIP On Saturdays, watch for special food and activity demonstrations.

By around 500 AD, native Hohokam peoples were developing advanced irrigation systems, and a thousand years later the Tohono O'odham were growing an extensive array of field crops, including wild greens. The arrival of the Spanish in the late seventeenth century introduced fruit trees—fig, quince, pomegranate, peach, and citrus—as well as Old World vegetables and grains to the area. (A recently completed

In the place where pre-historic Tucson was born, Mission Garden showcases crops and plants that have been grown over the course of 4,000 years. Along with trees and vegetables, the garden features a new acequia, *or Spanish-style aqueduct.*

Spanish Colonial *acequia*, or irrigation canal, is now a prominent feature of the garden.)

Subsequent waves of settlers, including Mexicans, Chinese, Anglos, and African Americans, brought in more crops, ranging from chilies to bitter melon and sweet potatoes. Since many traditional plants are seasonal, you never know exactly what you'll see when you visit. Run by the nonprofit Friends of Tucson's Birthplace, Mission Garden offers a variety of tours, special events, educational programs, and demonstrations throughout the year.

Mission Garden is the first project in an ambitious plan known as Tucson Origins Heritage Park, which eventually aims to re-create the entire San Agustín Mission complex that once stood nearby.

27 PHARMACEUTICAL FANTASIA

Where can you find laxative salts, liquid cocaine bottles, and fertility syrups?

If you've ever wondered where the "Rx" symbol for pharmacies originated or what your great-grandparents may have relied on to boost their fertility, or if you just want to step behind the counter of an old-fashioned soda fountain, head to the History of Pharmacy Museum on the University of Arizona campus.

Situated in two College of Pharmacy buildings with many of its eye-catching exhibits spread out in various hallways, the museum displays thousands of rare and unusual items related to pharmaceuticals, mostly dating from the mid-nineteenth to mid-twentieth centuries. Don't miss the re-created old-time drugstore where, alongside ice cream and photo supplies, giant bottles of booze were sold as legal medicinals during Prohibition.

One notable display is devoted to the Upjohn Pharmacy collection that once spent fifteen years on Disneyland's Main Street; it's considered one of the finest assemblages of antique pharmacy items in the world (including exquisite Italian olive oil vats from the late 1700s). Others showcase a fascinating array of medicinal herbs, elixirs, tinctures, and tonics. Back in the day, you could stop in to your local apothecary shop and pick up some liquid cocaine, extract of opium, heroin hydrate,

One of the museum's most unusual items is a jar containing bank robber John Dillinger's used chewing gum, salvaged from the underside of a Tucson drugstore lunch counter.

The College of Pharmacy Museum at the University of Arizona is the place to see an array of early pharmaceuticals—including exotic medicinal herbs, tinctures, tonics, fertility boosters, and liquid cocaine—as well as rare porcelain containers and re-creations of old-time drugstores.

HISTORY OF PHARMACY MUSEUM

WHAT A peek into pharmaceuticals past

WHERE 1295 N. Martin Ave.

COST Free

PRO TIP Guided tours are available Monday through Friday all year except when UA is not in session (call 520-626-1042).

swamp root, or even cigarettes intended to alleviate asthma. Or perhaps you might have been game to try a fig syrup fertility booster that promised a "baby in every bottle." And where did that Rx icon originate? From an ancient alchemical symbol meaning "take" (recipe), which simply resembled those letters.

While the displays are primarily intended to help immerse pharmacy students in the history of their field, the public is welcome to tour. Curator-guided tours are highly recommended, but self-guided tours are also available. The museum will soon be expanding to recognize the future of pharmacy as well as its past.

28 CELEBRITY LOCOMOTIVE

Where can kids play conductor on a real steam train engine?

Just down the way from Tucson's restored Historic Train Depot, which now serves as the city's Amtrak station, stands the powerful 1900s-era Locomotive #1673, which during its service hauled freight more than a million miles for the Southern Pacific. The steam engine even took a celebrity turn by appearing in the 1955 movie musical *Oklahoma!*, which was filmed near Tucson. The engine then took a final ride into the city to celebrate the seventy-fifth anniversary of the railroad's arrival here in 1880 and enjoyed a well-earned retirement, moving to a park and then to its current location in the year 2000.

Ensconced in a cage a few hundred feet down the tracks from the train station, however, even the mighty engine is easy to overlook. Still, train-crazy kids with parents in tow give it plenty of love, clambering up into the cab to ring the bell, pull levers, and play conductor. Docents from the little Southern Arizona Transportation Museum, located nearby, are there to supervise and answer questions; many are retired railway workers themselves.

The museum, also well worth a stop, is a restoration of the Southern Pacific Railroad Depot's records building and is crammed with colorful memorabilia and exhibits devoted to local railway history. Tucson's trains proved to be not just a vital link in a network that helped build the West, but they

SOUTHERN PACIFIC LOCOMOTIVE #1673

WHAT A railway landmark

WHERE 414 N. Toole Ave.

COST Free

PRO TIP Nearby statues of Wyatt Earp and Doc Holliday mark the spot where they gunned down Frank Stilwell in 1882.

Fresh from a role in the 1955 film Oklahoma!, *Southern Pacific Locomotive #1673 made its final ride to Tucson and now rests near the city's Historic Train Depot. The engine, which logged more than a million miles before retirement, is often open to the public.*

were also the crucial factor in the city's transformation from a small isolated town that was previously reachable only by horse and wagon. The Historic Train Depot, which originally dates from 1907, boasts polished wooden seating and vintage photos that grace the ticket office and classic waiting room area. All told, the complex of train depot and museum helps evoke the nostalgia and romance of Tucson's railway legacy—but perhaps none as much as Southern Pacific Locomotive #1673.

The Transportation Museum hosts an annual Silver Spike Celebration that commemorates the arrival of the railroad each March 20.

29 SWAP TILL YOU DROP

Where can I buy or sell just about anything?

Are you in the market to buy a used pipe wrench, an old coin collection, a 1950s-era table lamp, some outdated but cool-looking maps, a distressed leather jacket, some fresh garden vegetables, an antique credenza, a flip-up cell phone, some hand-knitted baby mittens, a seldom-used set of Waterford crystal, a hand-carved kachina doll, some flashy turquoise jewelry, a Webster's unabridged dictionary, a world globe still displaying the Soviet Union, a vinyl recording of Patsy Cline's *Greatest Hits*, or an almost-good-as-new fax machine?

Are you trying to sell a used pipe wrench, an old coin collection, a 1950s-era table lamp, some outdated but cool-looking maps, a distressed leather jacket, some fresh garden vegetables, an antique credenza, a flip-up cell phone, some hand-knitted baby mittens, a seldom-used set of Waterford crystal, a hand-carved kachina doll, some flashy turquoise jewelry, a Webster's unabridged dictionary, a world globe still displaying the Soviet Union, a vinyl recording of Patsy Cline's *Greatest Hits*, or an almost-good-as-new fax machine?

Then you need to know about the Tanque Verde Swap Meet, which takes place every weekend and where eager-to-unload sellers meet bargain-hungry buyers in a marriage made in Tucson. In business since 1975, the Swap Meet devotes nineteen acres of open air to sellers, who get there on a first-come, first-served basis, and another eleven acres to parking. Many families make a day (or evening) of it: there are

---

A number of local businesses, including Mac's Indian Jewelry, Kent's Tools, and University Perfumes, got their start by renting tables at the Swap Meet.

You can buy or sell just about anything at the Tanque Verde Swap Meet, where vendors set up shop at tables and buyers come to browse, maybe to find a good deal on an old Patsy Cline record, an antique credenza, or a used pipe wrench.

TANQUE VERDE SWAP MEET

WHAT Acres of stuff to buy or sell

WHERE 4100 S. Palo Verde Rd.

COST Free entry for buyers; $15–$20 per day for sellers

PRO TIP Open Fridays 3 to 11 p.m.; Saturdays 7 a.m. to 11 p.m.; Sundays 7 a.m. to 3 p.m.

kids' rides and activities, plenty of foods to snack and picnic on (tacos, raspados, burgers, frybread, pizza, nachos, ice cream, cotton candy . . .), and cold soda or beer to drink while you're dickering. You can even have your hair cut or braided, get a tattoo, or have your ears pierced. It's a one-stop shop, and you never know what you'll find. So come on down!

DESERT SNOW PLAY

What's the country's southernmost ski resort?

Tucson isn't exactly known for its winter sports, since the city itself seldom sees more than a dusting of snow. But Mt. Lemmon—at 9,157 feet, the highest peak in the Santa Catalina range just north of Tucson—is a different story. The mountain gets an average of fifteen feet of snowfall annually, providing nearby skiing to any Tucsonans who want to delve beyond more typical desert seasonal sporting activities such as playing golf or tennis.

MT. LEMMON SKI VALLEY

WHAT A Tucson ski resort

WHERE 10300 Ski Run Rd., Mt. Lemmon

COST All-day adult lift tickets, $47; ages 12 and under, $27

PRO TIP Open Thursday to Monday 9 a.m. to 4 p.m., December to March, weather permitting.

Mt. Lemmon Ski Valley has roots going back a century to the World War I era, when journalist Lowell Thomas and some cohorts created the Sahuaro Ski Club in Tucson, a partially tongue-in-cheek society whose logo depicted a skier entangled with a saguaro cactus. But with the aid of a jerry-built rope tow (an old car with its tires removed), the ski club forged ahead with its quixotic venture, and the southernmost ski resort in the country was born.

Today, skiers and snowboarders can ride three lifts and choose among more than twenty runs for beginner, intermediate, and advanced levels. Ski Valley has a vertical drop of 950 feet, while the longest run is 8,500 feet. Equipment rentals and ski and snowboard lessons are available. The Catalina Highway up Mt. Lemmon often closes after a snowfall until the roads are cleared, but even if it's open, carry tire chains from fall to spring and fill up with gas before you go.

It may be sunny in Tucson, but high up on 9,157-foot Mt. Lemmon in the Catalinas, just north of the city, some folks might be hitting the slopes at the country's southernmost ski resort.

In warmer months, the Mt. Lemmon ski lift offers scenic rides from its base at 8,200 feet to the summit, a thirty-minute excursion with panoramic views and chances to spot wildlife.

What brought a notorious New York crime boss to Tucson?

Crime boss Joe Bonanno, once head of one of the New York Mafia's Five Families and widely believed to be a model for the epic *Godfather* book and movies, spent his final decades in Tucson and is buried in a crypt in the Holy Hope Cemetery here. From the time he took over the Bonanno crime family in 1931, he was notorious for his roles in narcotics trafficking, prostitution, loan sharking, and bookmaking.

Often dubbed "Joe Bananas"—a name he despised—Bonanno left Brooklyn for Tucson in 1968, banished by his fellow Mafiosi following his divisive "Banana War" for control of the New York crime syndicate. Bonanno already had deep Tucson ties, though, having developed business interests and sending his children to school here. His son, Bill, also heavily involved in organized crime, called Tucson home much of his life and was a key source for the 1971 Gay Talese best-seller *Honor Thy Father*. He is also said to have helped inspire the *Godfather* character Michael Corleone.

While Joe Bonanno lived a relatively quiet semi-retirement in Tucson, he spent a total of twenty-two months in prison in the 1980s on obstruction of justice and contempt charges. He also lived under constant threat of death for allegedly violating the Mafia code of omertà (silence) after publishing his 1983 autobiography, *A Man of Honor*. But he lived to be ninety-

---

JOE BONANNO CRYPT

WHAT A mobster's burial site

WHERE 3555 N. Oracle Rd.

COST Free

PRO TIP Look for the large monument directly ahead of the cemetery entrance; the crypt is to the rear of it.

Crime boss Joe Bonanno, banished by the Mafia from his New York base, spent the last several decades of his life in Tucson, mostly living a low-key existence. He is buried in the Holy Hope Cemetery here (pictured).

three years old, dying from heart failure in 2002. Bill Bonanno died in Tucson in 2008.

According to newspaper accounts at the time, Joe Bonanno's friends and neighbors found him to be a "consummate gentleman, extremely charming." In the words of one, "I wouldn't find a better neighbor." The inscription on his crypt reads "God Family Tradition."

Bonanno's funeral mass at Saints Peter and Paul Roman Catholic Church in Tucson drew some five hundred mourners, many with alleged Mafia family ties.

32 TUCSON'S PAST ON PARADE

Where can you find fringed-top surreys, historic carriages, and the city's first garbage truck?

Many Tucsonans have attended the annual rodeo (La Fiesta de los Vaqueros). Many have watched the Rodeo Parade, which takes place during Rodeo Week and is billed as the world's longest non-mechanized parade. Far fewer have visited the sprawling Rodeo Museum, which is open only January through March each year. The museum spans several buildings, including a 1930s adobe, some barns, and an old airplane hangar, and showcases more than one hundred historic vehicles mostly run by horsepower—that is, real horses.

Old-time-movie buffs may recognize the "surreys with the fringe on top" that were featured in the 1955 movie *Oklahoma!*—which was actually filmed south of Tucson. Other carriages and wagons on display once transported Hollywood stars Ava Gardner and Maureen O'Hara in their movies, the industrialist-philanthropist Andrew Carnegie, and the ill-fated Mexican Emperor Maximilian and Empress Carlotta during their coronation in the 1860s. Somewhat less glamorous but still of interest are Tucson's first garbage truck, its first chemical fire wagon, a cotton seeder, a police paddy wagon, stagecoaches, and wagons made by Frederick Ronstadt, Tucson-born singer Linda Ronstadt's grandfather.

Duncan Renaldo, who played the Cisco Kid in a TV Western back in the 1950s, donated a horse trailer to the museum's collection.

Tucson's Rodeo Parade Museum is lined with carriages and other vehicles that have starred in the world's longest non-motorized parade, an event held since 1925 during the city's annual Rodeo Week.

The museum also depicts Tucson as it was at the turn of the twentieth century, with a typical blacksmith shop, a saddle shop, a jail, a saloon, a birthing center, and a mercantile. A toy train exhibit recreating 1880s Tucson, complete with sound effects of cattle, saloon music, and mission bells, includes a G scale model steam locomotive. Another exhibit displays artifacts from the El Conquistador Hotel, Tucson's first luxury lodging, which attracted Hollywood celebrities in the 1930s. There's much more—you just have to remember to visit in winter.

RODEO PARADE MUSEUM

WHAT Tucson's past on parade

WHERE 4823 S. Sixth Ave.

COST $12; seniors, $9; children, $2

PRO TIP The museum is closed the day of the Rodeo Parade.

AN ABUNDANCE OF AIRCRAFT

Where do mothballed military planes go to die (or rest)?

It's officially known as the 309th Aerospace Maintenance and Regeneration Group (AMARG) at Tucson's Davis-Monthan Air Force Base, but just about everyone calls it the Boneyard. With more than four thousand mothballed military and NASA planes stored in neat rows on the city's southeastern reaches, it holds all U.S. military aircraft that are removed from service, and—at 2,600 acres—is the largest such facility in the world. Some planes are repaired for display, and some donate their spare parts and are then scrapped, while others are refurbished and readied to fly again if needed.

Opened after World War II, the Boneyard has been the repository for just about every type of excess or outmoded bomber, jet fighter, helicopter, or cargo plane from all branches of the military: B-1s, B-29s, B-52s, F-4s, F-14 Tomcats, A-10 Warthogs, C-74s, C-130s, and C-141 Starlifters, among many others. Hundreds of on-site "Boneyard Wranglers," as they call themselves, see to the maintenance, restoration, and, if necessary, destruction of the aircraft. (With Soviet satellites monitoring from above, for instance, many B-52s were dramatically demolished at the Boneyard following strategic arms limitation treaties in the 1970s.)

Boneyard tours are operated solely through the auspices of the adjoining, privately run Pima Air & Space Museum,

---

While Tucson's dry desert heat and sparse rains ward off mold and rust, many Boneyard planes are covered by white plastic shields to protect them from sun and other elements.

Thousands of mothballed U.S. military and NASA planes are neatly lined up at Tucson's Boneyard, the largest such facility in the world. Tours are available through the adjacent Pima Air & Space Museum.

THE BONEYARD

WHAT Miles of mothballed aircraft

WHERE 6000 E. Valencia Rd.

COST $20

PRO TIP You may carry only a small camera, purse, or belt pack on the tour.

which itself houses some of the Boneyard's most historic aircraft. The narrated bus tours last ninety minutes, and everyone must stay onboard throughout. Due to security concerns, ten-day advance reservations are required, as is receiving clearance from the Air Force base. Adults (age sixteen and up) must furnish documentation—federal- or state-issued photo ID for U.S. citizens; passports for non-citizens—along with other information. Complete instructions are available on the Pima Air & Space Museum website (pimaair.org).

34 BACKSTAGE AT A MOVIE PALACE

Where did John Wayne sit when he went to the flicks?

After standing empty for twenty-five years, the 1930s-era Fox Tucson Theatre, Tucson's first movie palace, underwent a $14 million renovation from 1995 to 2007, restoring it to its onetime Art Deco glory. A former house manager, Tom Skinner, now leads free once-a-month in-season (September to May) backstage tours of the Fox for the public, and they're laced with fascinating historical tidbits about the films and musicians that have played there.

The night the Fox movie palace opened in 1930, three thousand people—a tenth of Tucson's population at the time and more than twice the theater's capacity—showed up to attend the film *Chasing Rainbows*, one of the first talking musicals. The "Southwest Art Deco" architecture and décor were much the same as they are today, with "zigzag" patterns, sunburst iconography, and Egyptian touches throughout (King

FOX THEATRE BACKSTAGE TOURS

WHAT Intimate look at a vintage theater

WHERE 17 W. Congress St.

COST Free (donations accepted)

PRO TIP The tour includes several staircases and is not handicap accessible.

When restorers went to work on the high-hung central chandelier, they found a dead pigeon and a half-eaten hot dog inside; how the latter got there is a mystery.

The renovated Fox Tucson Theatre, the city's first movie palace and major concert hall, is open for monthly tours that take you backstage and up into the seats where John Wayne once settled in to watch his favorite flicks.

Tut was big then). The stunning central chandelier that hangs high above the main floor is original and serves as the theater's iconic symbol.

John Wayne, who starred in Western films made at Old Tucson Studios outside town, is said to have sat in seats 17–19 ZZ at the very end of the top row of the loge; the seats there are double wide, enough for two people. (A starstruck former city mayor donated enough money to have his name engraved on "Wayne's" armrest.) A walk around the stage gives you a sense of what it's like to appear before nearly 1,200 people—albeit while playing to empty seats. In the basement, meanwhile, are dressing rooms where the corridor walls have been autographed by featured musicians: Janis Joplin, Gary Puckett, and the Kingston Trio among them. Besides live music acts, the Fox still screens classic films and has recently acquired a Wurlitzer organ, perfect for accompanying the occasional old-time silent movie.

35

SECLUDED SETTING

Which midtown neighborhood resembles a nature preserve?

Just off busy Broadway Boulevard a few minutes' drive east of downtown Tucson lies a secluded, gorgeously landscaped neighborhood, complete with winding streets that curve past some of the city's most attractive homes. The streets loop around five mini-parks that harbor a riot of vegetation— towering saguaro cacti, giant agaves, stately palm trees—in a desert-like setting; an arroyo runs through part of it. It's like entering a nature preserve in the middle of the city, yet thousands drive by it every day without even knowing it's there.

The Colonia Solana ("Sunny Colony") historic neighborhood, designed in 1928 by Stephen Child, a protégé of noted landscape architect Frederick Law Olmstead, was one of Arizona's first suburban subdivisions when it was a long buggy ride east of downtown (though urban Tucson has long since enveloped it and it's now in the central part of the city). In keeping with its desert theme, Child's design is informal and non-symmetrical, in sharp contrast to the formal layout of its contemporary subdivision just to the north, El Encanto Estates. Colonia Solana is also notable for the size of its housing lots, which are considerably larger than almost anywhere

Singer and Tucson native Linda Ronstadt lived in a walled 4,100-square-foot 1928 Mediterranean-style home at 147 S. Avenida de Palmas in Colonia Solana for twenty-two years before selling it in 2016.

The lush Colonia Solana historic neighborhood in midtown Tucson, designed by a protégé of noted landscape architect Frederick Law Olmstead, resembles a nature preserve in the middle of the city.

COLONIA SOLANA

WHAT A midtown desert sanctuary

WHERE E. Broadway Blvd. and Country Club Rd.

COST Free

PRO TIP Convenient entry points off East Broadway are on South Avenida de Palmas and East Via Palos Verdes.

else in Tucson. The 120 or so homes there are an attractive mix of architectural styles— Spanish Colonial Revival, mid-century ranch, Territorial, and Mediterranean, among others— designed by prominent local architects of the day such as Roy Place and Arthur T. Brown. The neighborhood's well-manicured gardens, patios, and fountains enhance the ambiance of the natural setting, and it's all been beautifully kept up.

36

A CLASSY CLASSIC NEIGHBORHOOD

What makes these the "Enchanted Estates"?

Like Colonia Solana, its nearly adjacent fellow historic neighborhood, El Encanto ("Enchanted") Estates dates from 1928 and harbors some of the city's most architecturally rich older homes—seemingly a world apart from the traffic of the busy streets that whiz past its entrances just a short distance away. And also like Colonia Solana, El Encanto started out as a suburban subdivision of Tucson, at the time a small city of just over thirty thousand people, before urban sprawl enveloped it on all sides. Its closest neighbor back then was the glamorous El Conquistador Hotel, which drew Hollywood stars and other well-known figures to its doors before falling on hard times and being torn down in 1968.

While El Encanto displays less of the lush desert vegetation that makes Colonia Solana so distinctive, its attractive streets are lined with towering palms. The neighborhood is an enclave unto itself. El Encanto's quiet streets are laid out in a symmetrical bull's-eye pattern with a small circular park in the center and roads extending out from it like spokes on a wheel, leading to a ring road surrounded by more lots. Its 140 or so homes represent a number of architectural styles, including Spanish Colonial, Early California, Mission Revival, Moroccan, Italian, and Pueblo Revival, and were designed by some of the

El Encanto's streets all sport Spanish names, such as Calle de Amistad ("Friendship Street") and Calle Belleza ("Beauty Street"), that were chosen in a contest; the winners each received five dollars.

The historic palm-lined El Encanto Estates seems a world apart from its bordering traffic-filled streets. The 1928-era neighborhood contains homes representing a number of architectural styles designed by some of Tucson's top architects of the time.

most prominent local architects of the day: Josias Joesler, Anne Jackson Rysdale, and Arthur T. Brown, among others. El Encanto was added to the National Register of Historic Places in 1988.

EL ENCANTO ESTATES

WHAT A classic midtown neighborhood

WHERE Roughly bounded by E. Broadway Blvd., E. Fifth St., N. Campbell Ave., and N. Country Club Rd.

COST Free

PRO TIP There are six entry points from the surrounding streets.

37 A CHICANO MUSIC LEGEND

How did Tucson help shape the life of Lalo Guerrero?

Known as the "father of Chicano music," Eduardo (Lalo) Guerrero was born in Tucson's historic Barrio Viejo, where he grew up before moving to California and gaining fame as a singer and songwriter. But while in Tucson, to which he returned often until his death at age eighty-eight in 2005, he learned to play guitar and piano, formed various singing groups, and managed to survive what he called a rough neighborhood. "Police never even dared go into that area it was so rough," he recalled in an interview. "That's why they called it Barrio Libre" (Free Neighborhood).

Guerrero's early résumé included vocal stints at downtown Tucson's landmark El Charro restaurant, where he earned five dollars a week plus another five to ten dollars in tips; he later attributed his relatively high singing voice to the strains of crooning nine hours a night there. At age seventeen, Guerrero wrote his most enduring song, "Canción Mexicana," an homage to a homeland he had not yet visited. During his career, he recorded more than seven hundred songs and twenty albums while delving into many different musical styles, ranging from mariachi tunes to popular parodies to politically charged songs known as "corridos."

LALO GUERRERO'S CHILDHOOD NEIGHBORHOOD

WHAT Where the musical legend grew up

WHERE Barrio Viejo, just south of downtown

COST Free

PRO TIP Guerrero was born where South Meyer Avenue meets Simpson Street, but his house is now gone.

The Barrio Viejo—where the "father of Chicano music," Lalo Guerrero, grew up—has changed considerably since his childhood in the 1920s. But, as this renovated adobe demonstrates, the neighborhood still retains its Sonoran-Spanish flavor.

Guerrero inspired musicians such as Los Lobos, Ry Cooder, and Linda Ronstadt, and his work was featured in the 1978 stage musical and subsequent film *Zoot Suit*. While Barrio Viejo is now largely gentrified and his childhood home is no longer standing, Guerrero's legacy still lingers in the "Free Neighborhood" where his mother taught him to play guitar at age nine—and launched a musical legend.

Guerrero was named a National Folk Treasure by the Smithsonian Institution in 1980 and awarded the Presidential Medal of the Arts in 1997, the first Mexican-American to be so honored.

³⁸ FARCICAL FOLLIES

Where can you find wacky takes on old game shows?

It's Tucson's longest-running monthly comedy show. Since its debut in 2011, the hilarious Retro Game Show Night has parodied and pilloried a raft of vintage shows with sketches like "Sassword," "Wheel of Misfortune," "The Mismatch Game," "Family Fuss," and "Hollywood(ish) Squares" while serving as a showcase for wacky local comic talents. Quick-witted comedians like bawdy drag queen Tempest DuJour and, more recently, "Chatty Kathee" (Missy Paschke)—a veteran of the Tucson improv scene who brings manic energy to the stage—set the pace. Panelists include local "celebrities" like QiQo (who "can't wait to launch his line of vegan swimwear"), Elena Sanchez (who "can't wait to get her test results back"), and Uncle Herb (who is "sleeping on your sofa forever"). More normally "straight" well-known locals have also been lured into appearing, perhaps to their regret.

Contestants include eager audience members who have signed up to play—or, sometimes to their surprise, have been unknowingly signed up by their friends. Meanwhile, the standing-room-only audiences come primed to whoop and holler as the hosts engage in rapid-fire repartee with those on stage and in the seats. "Splash Zone" ticketholders, in reserved seating near the front, are the most likely targets. One thing you can count on is that once you've experienced Retro's take on them, those old game shows will never seem quite the same.

Retro Game Show Night, Tucson's longest-running monthly comedy show, presents wacky take-offs on vintage TV game shows, but the real stars are its quick-witted hosts, such as Chatty Kathee (pictured) and the hilarious drag queen Tempest du Jour.

RETRO GAME SHOW NIGHT

WHAT Wacky take on TV game shows

WHERE Hotel Congress, 311 E. Congress St.

COST $10–$12

PRO TIP Doors open at 6 p.m.; arrive early if you don't have a reserved seat.

Producer David Hoffman says the show was originally designed to bring customers into a now-closed restaurant before moving to Club Congress: "We never thought we'd be around this long."

<u>39</u> HISTORY ON HORSEBACK

Where can you sleep in the Pancho Villa Villa?

John Wayne slept there. So did two American presidents, Franklin D. Roosevelt (along with wife Eleanor) and Lyndon B. Johnson, and a vice president, Hubert H. Humphrey. Toss in another Hollywood star or two (Joan Crawford, old-time movie cowboy Tom Mix), some famous authors, Zane Grey and Margaret Mitchell among them, and a U.S. Supreme Court justice (William O. Douglas), and you realize that Rancho de la Osa has had a pretty impressive guest list.

As if that wasn't history enough, William Clayton, architect of the Marshall Plan, which helped rebuild Europe after World War II, drafted the document in one of the houses. Another of the buildings on the property is thought to be the oldest in continuous use in Arizona, dating back to the late 1700s, when Jesuit missionaries ran a trading post there. And while Mexican revolutionary Pancho Villa was never a guest at the Rancho, he did attack it in 1915, an event memorialized by

RANCHO DE LA OSA

WHAT A historic borderlands ranch

WHERE 1 La Osa Ranch Rd., Sasabe

COST $185 to $335 per person

PRO TIP Sasabe has a lone store and bar open Saturdays only, 1 to 6 p.m.

The ranch's eighteen adobe rooms, many named for its famous guests and specifically requested by repeat visitors, are furnished with Mexican antiques and wood-burning fireplaces.

The hacienda-style Rancho de la Osa near the Mexican border has hosted a number of famous guests and features activities such as horseback riding in a national wildlife refuge, hiking in the Baboquivari Mountains, and touring the border by ATV or electric bicycle.

the room delightfully titled Pancho Villa Villa. No wonder Rancho de la Osa lays claim to being Arizona's most historic ranch.

Well off the beaten track in tiny Sasabe, Arizona, just a mile from the Mexican border, the 590-acre guest ranch, still an architectural gem, can be reached by car from Tucson within an hour and a half. Activities are all inclusive and focus on horseback riding. Trails lead into the adjacent Buenos Aires National Wildlife Refuge, and you can also ride to the border or tour it by ATV or electric bicycle. Other activities include hiking in the Baboquivari Mountains, photographing landscapes and wildlife, exploring petroglyphs, practicing your sport shooting and archery, and dining on tasty food served communal style. Managers Ross and Lynne Knox are personable hosts: Ross is an authentic cowboy and wrangler—whose talents extend to reciting cowboy poetry—while Lynn oversees the many activities.

⁴⁰ MOVABLE ART

Can trash also be treasure?

As the saying goes, "One man's trash is another man's treasure." Or, in the case of artist Ned Schaper, aka Mat Bevel, his trash is his treasure. Noting that since "trash is the great medium of our age," Schaper believes it would be a shame to let it go to waste, as it were. And so, the "Junk Evangelist" has filled his longtime Museum of Kinetic Art in Tucson with more than 150 crazily creative sculptures that he's fashioned entirely from discarded and recycled items: everything from pinwheels to old musical instruments, broken toys to bike parts, ironing boards to scrap metal, ski poles to chandeliers.

Kinetic art is art that moves, and so the sculptures twirl and spin, and as they do they whir, clank, and hum. Some light up, and others look like fish or birds or butterflies, but mostly they look like something from another galaxy. When Schaper starts a sculpture, he doesn't have a plan in mind—it just comes together. "Everything wants to be used," he contends. "Beveldom," as he calls it, is where "lost objects find a magical new life."

The artworks also serve as props and sets in Schaper's Surrealistic Pop Science Theater productions, in which his alter ego, Mat Bevel, offers humorous, entertaining lessons about science and technology, employing music and poetry in the process. As sole creative director and performer of the Mat Bevel Institute—the "Institute," he has said, gives it the imprimatur of seriousness—he's had successful one-man exhibitions at the Tucson Museum of Art and worked with

Schaper, whose educational background is in physics, developed his Mat Bevel character while performing avant-garde street theater.

"Junk Evangelist" Ned Schaper (aka Mat Bevel) uses art objects made from trash as props in his Surrealistic Pop Science Theatre productions, as well as at his Museum of Kinetic Art in Tucson.

schools on developing courses for students on creative problem-solving. The Junk Evangelist, it seems, has converted a lot of Tucsonans to the magical world of Beveldom.

MAT BEVEL'S MUSEUM OF KINETIC ART

WHAT Amazing junk sculptures that move

WHERE 3113 E. Columbia St.

COST $12 for private tour

PRO TIP The museum is currently open only for private tours and special events.

FADED GLORY

What's so miraculous about the Miracle Mile?

There was a time, back in the mid-twentieth century, when motorists driving down Tucson's Miracle Mile wouldn't have wondered how it got that name. As the northern gateway to the city, the Miracle Mile was the center of a neon-lit business district that thrived with the automobile tourism boom that swept the United States from the 1940s through the 1960s. The Miracle Mile, actually a 1.75-mile-long artery, boasted a riot of illuminated signs beckoning travelers to have a meal, shop for souvenirs, and stay at new palm-fringed motels and motor courts with swimming pools. Tucson—which actively promoted the new car culture—became a regular stop for folks driving across the country.

MIRACLE MILE

WHAT A relic of 1950s car culture

WHERE Interstate 10 east to Oracle Rd.

COST Free

PRO TIP The area is still a bit seedy, so take normal precautions at night.

Construction began in 1937 on Miracle Mile, which incorporated one of the nation's first landscaped medians. Celebrated as a model of safety, it soon acquired its "Miracle" moniker. (A similarly named stretch of Los Angeles' Wilshire Boulevard may have offered inspiration.) But with the arrival of Interstate 10 in the 1960s, which provided a bypass around the city, the Miracle Mile lost its luster and began a long decline that eventually saw the area devolve into poverty and crime. The name itself became kind of a sardonic joke.

Tucson's "Miracle Mile" was so named back in the mid-twentieth century because it was a model of safety, as well as the neon-lit gateway to the city. While its glory has faded, some signs like that of the old Ghost Ranch Lodge, designed by artist Georgia O'Keefe, have survived.

But things may be changing. The Ghost Ranch Lodge & Restaurant, whose ox-skull sign was designed by artist Georgia O'Keeffe, has been converted into affordable senior housing. The old Monterey Court has been reborn as a music and dining venue as well as an artists' lair. And it's worth a drive over to Miracle Mile just to see the remaining neon signage and imagine how miraculous it all must once have seemed.

The entire Miracle Mile district—including nearby stretches of Oracle Road, Drachman Street, and Stone and Main Avenues—was recently listed on the National Register of Historic Places.

What's a Franklin, anyway?

Car restorer Thomas Hubbard loved Franklin autos—so much so that he kept buying the classic early-twentieth-century vehicles from 1950 until his death in 1993. Housed in historic adobes in a residential area in northern Tucson, the Franklin Auto Museum showcases Hubbard's nearly thirty-strong collection of Franklins, which were assembled in Syracuse, New York, from 1902 until 1934, when they fell victim to a Depression-era downturn.

Hubbard's own infatuation with Franklins dated from 1933, when his parents purchased that year's model. At age eight, he was already hooked. While mostly a forgotten brand now—they were named for businessman Herbert H. Franklin, who along with engineer John Wilkinson was the driving force behind the vintage cars—some 150,000 Franklins were produced over more than thirty years, and only a few thousand still survive.

FRANKLIN AUTO MUSEUM

WHAT Vintage Franklin automobiles

WHERE 3420 N. Vine Ave. (near Kleindale Rd. intersection)

COST $10; seniors, $8; teens/students, $5

PRO TIP The museum closes from Memorial Day until mid-October.

The museum's collection, the largest of its kind in the world, includes Herbert Franklin's personal automobile, a Franklin Model 153 (which dates from 1929–1931 because the automaker brought it into the company garage each year for updates). A 1931 Franklin Model 153 Sport Phaeton was purchased for the then-princely sum of $6,500 by a twenty-one-year-old looking to impress his bride on their honeymoon. And a 1905 Franklin Model A Runabout is a post-Hubbard museum acquisition, purchased with funds from his endowment. The museum also includes an extensive library of Franklin Auto history.

Some 30 classic Franklin automobiles, produced between 1902 and 1934, are on display at the Franklin Auto Museum in Tucson, the largest such collection in the world. With advanced cooling systems and brilliant design, they were favorites of pilots Charles Lindbergh and Amelia Earhart.

With its air-cooled "airplane-type" engines, Franklin emphasized its aviation tie-ins and counted famed pilots Charles Lindbergh and Amelia Earhart among the cars' proud owners.

VILLAGE SQUARE AMBIANCE (page 184)

HIGH FLYERS (page 156)

COLOSSAL HIDEOUT (page 136)

SIGNS OF LIFE (page 10)

HOBNOBBING WITH THE SNOBS (page 30)

STEINFELD
MANSION

SNAKING AROUND (page 142)

GOING PEACEFULLY POSTAL (page 122)

JOHN DILLINGER'S BAD DAY (page 40)

ARIZONA'S FIRST COMMERCIAL VINEYARD (page 36)

A MOVIE STAR'S RETREAT (page 48)

PHARMACEUTICAL FANTASIA (page 54)

A GLIMPSE BACK IN TIME (page 166)

HISTORY ON HORSEBACK (page 78)

A CLASSY CLASSIC NEIGHBORHOOD (page 72)

CARNE, POR FAVOR

Where can you buy beef ready to grill for tacos?

Without some advance prep on how exactly things are supposed to work there, those walking into a Tucson *carniceria*—a Mexican-style meat market—may understandably be a little confused. There may also be a language barrier for those who don't speak Spanish. But don't let any of that put you off, or you might miss one of the great carnivorous treats of living in Tucson. One of the best *carnicerias* in the city, Beef Master, located just off Interstate 10, is a good case in point.

Approaching the market, you can't miss the big charcoal grill fired up out front. You may see slices of steak and green onions waiting to be grilled, and your inclination may be to ask the grill master for piles of tacos. That won't work. Instead, go inside the market and head straight to the refrigerated meat section, where dozens of chuck steaks of different sizes await. Some will be marinated, some not. What you may not notice is that, while packaged and resembling roasts, the meats are actually pre-sliced very thin, so that they can easily be peeled off and placed on the grill.

On the nearby shelves are selections of tortillas (both corn and flour), salsas, beverages, and other possible accompaniments to your meal. Pay for your items at the cashier and go back outside. Now you're ready for the grill

---

You can also assemble your tacos yourself on the spot if you've purchased tortillas and salsa, but since there aren't many places to sit, most customers make them at home.

Smoke rises from the grill in front of Beef Master carniceria, a Mexican-style meat market in South Tucson. After purchasing your thinly sliced steak inside, you can return outside where the grill master will cook it up and produce delicious fillings for tacos.

master to take over. He'll peel off the steak slices, place them on the grill (along with onions and tortillas if you choose), and within a few minutes, depending on the wait, you'll have some of the most delicious takeout you can find in Tucson.

BEEF MASTER CARNICERIA

WHAT Meat for tacos sold and grilled

WHERE 527 W. 29th St.

COST Cost of meats plus $3 tip for the grill master

PRO TIP Get there early, before mealtimes if possible, to avoid the crowds.

<u>44</u> SPEED DEMONS

Where can I race high-performance go-karts in Tucson?

There's no mystery as to why the folks behind Autobahn named it after the freewheeling German superhighways where speed limits are virtually nonexistent. "Our philosophy is simple," they proclaim. "No speed limits!" Actually—since this is a go-kart raceway and not a proving ground for amateur Mercedes vs. BMW racers—there is a practical limit: the go-karts can reach speeds of up to fifty miles per hour. But that provides plenty of excitement for the adults and kids who take to the indoor track and race against family, friends, or other competitors. Autobahn has two tracks: Monaco and Le Mans. Adults (ages thirteen and up) get to go fourteen laps around the track, while kids aged eight to twelve, who ride in specially made junior karts reaching speeds up to twenty-five miles per hour, do twelve laps. The race ends when the leader crosses the finish line.

Autobahn's Italian-made Formula 1-style go-karts are propelled by high-performance electric engines and come

AUTOBAHN INDOOR SPEEDWAY

WHAT High-performance go-kart racing

WHERE 300 S. Toole Ave.

COST $19.99 for a single race; multi-race packages available

PRO TIP Wear closed-toed shoes and avoid loose-fitting clothing.

Junior racers must be at least forty-eight inches tall and eight years old; adults must be at least fifty-six inches tall and thirteen years old and weigh less than three hundred pounds.

High-performance Formula 1-style go-karts are ready for racing at Autobahn, where two tracks attract both junior racers and adults, who can reach speeds up to 50 mph at Arizona's largest indoor karting facility.

with plenty of safety features: dual-disk brakes, brake lights, roll bars, four-point safety harnesses, and helmets. And as the largest completely indoor karting facility in the state, with seventy thousand square feet, it's available for racing in all kinds of weather. You don't need a driver's license to compete (though you do have to sign a liability waiver, minors must bring in a signed waiver from a parent or guardian, and there are some height and weight restrictions). But first, you do need to find it. While it's near downtown, Autobahn is in an off-the-beaten-track location, in the same general area as the Rocks and Ropes indoor climbing gym.

107

LAST OF A BREED

Where can you find classic videos and a brew?

Video rental stores are rare enough in Tucson—there are fewer than a handful left in the city. But an independent video rental store stocked with thousands of film titles to meet just about any taste, complete with a roomy bar capable of quenching a movie lover's thirst after some exhaustive browsing, is unique.

Casa Video has been around for years, somehow managing to survive the onslaught of new technologies (and Netflix) that have led to the near-extinction of video stores nationally. But the Casa Film Bar, which opened in late 2015, has breathed new life into the operation. The attached bar contains plenty of seating, along with a selection of wines and a wide variety of craft beers: IPAs, ales, lagers, stouts, and porters, including several local brews on tap. Casa Video also offers free popcorn, which can't hurt beer sales. And to further entice customers, the bar shows movies and hosts periodic film trivia and game nights.

CASA VIDEO AND CASA FILM BAR

WHAT A video rental store with bar

WHERE 2905 E. Speedway Blvd.

COST Video rentals, $3–$5; beer, $4–$7

PRO TIP You can now order a video online for store pickup or mail delivery.

For bar munchies, you can order pizza from a local restaurant to be delivered to the bar; food trucks often pull up outside as well.

Tucson's Casa Video and Bar combines a huge selection of movie videos, DVDs, audio books, and video games with an attached bar offering craft beers and wine. Films include both new releases and classics, as well as foreign films, documentaries, and hard-to-find independent films.

Meanwhile, back in the video aisles, the eight-thousand-square-foot, two-level store practically groans under the weight of some fifty thousand titles, mostly videos, but also DVDs, audio books, and video games. Besides a host of new releases and classics, Casa Video has particularly good selections of hard-to-find foreign films, documentaries, and independent films, with a knowledgeable staff able to direct you to what you're looking for (or may not know you're looking for until you find it).

⁴⁶ A CITY WITHIN A CITY

Why is there a South Tucson?

It's a 1.2-square-mile enclave entirely surrounded by the city of Tucson. Its 5,600 or so inhabitants are served by their own mayor, city council, city manager, and police and fire departments. And remarkably, it's survived as its own city for more than eighty years—including fending off sporadic disputes with its giant neighbor and losing a multimillion-dollar personal injury lawsuit in 1978 that nearly led to its bankruptcy.

South Tucson was incorporated as a city in 1936, spearheaded by local property owners who wanted to avoid high big-city taxes when Tucson was preparing to annex the area south of what were then its borders. It lies about a mile south of downtown Tucson and harbors some three hundred businesses. The city's largely Hispanic heritage is celebrated in a variety of colorful outdoor tile murals, engaging Spanish-style architecture, and its motto, "The Pueblo Within a City."

South Tucson's big draw is its platter of Mexican restaurants, some among the best in the metro area (and which generate a substantial portion of city revenues). And while most Tucsonans would be hard-pressed to know exactly when they enter the enclave on their way to indulge in tacos or enchiladas, they probably don't care, as long as the margaritas keep flowing.

Among South Tucson's popular Mexican restaurants are Mi Nidito (1813 South Fourth Avenue), Guillermo's Double L Restaurant (1830 South Fourth Avenue), and Crossroads Restaurant (2602 South Fourth Avenue).

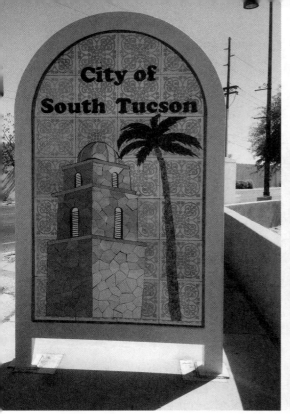

A sign welcomes visitors to South Tucson, a separate 1.2-square-mile city entirely surrounded by Tucson. The enclave is home to a number of popular Mexican restaurants as well as some colorful public murals and other artworks.

SOUTH TUCSON

WHAT An enclave within Tucson

WHERE 26th St. south to 40th St., and S. 12th Ave. east to the Union Pacific railroad tracks near S. 2nd Ave.

COST Free

PRO TIP South Sixth Avenue in South Tucson is noted for its Spanish-style architecture.

LYRICAL MYSTERY

Why did the Beatles sing about Tucson?

> *"JoJo left his home in Tucson, Arizona*
> *For some California grass . . .*
> *Get back, get back, get back to where you once belonged*
> *Get back, JoJo, go home . . . "*

So go some memorable lyrics from the Beatles' 1969 hit "Get Back." But why were the Beatles singing about Tucson? At the time "Get Back" was released, none of them had ever been to the city. Credit Paul McCartney, the main lyricist on the song.

Paul's wife, Linda—an accomplished photographer whom he had married that same year—had studied at the University of Arizona in the early 1960s. In 1979, the couple purchased a secluded 150-acre ranch near the Tanque Verde River on Tucson's northeast side. Linda could pursue her love of horseback riding in the Rincon Mountain foothills there and their four children could also swim and hike. Sadly, Linda died of breast cancer there in 1998.

Widespread speculation has it that "JoJo" was a reference to Linda's first husband, Joseph Melville See, but McCartney has denied that, mysteriously claiming that JoJo was an imaginary "half man, half woman" character. The refrain "Get back to where you once belonged" is yet another source of speculation, perhaps referring to the Beatles' attempt to get back to their roots and overcome their well-documented feuds at the time, centered around Paul, John Lennon, and

McCartney once suggested that the song was originally intended to parody British politicians' and the public's increasingly racist attitudes toward Pakistani immigrants.

Years after exhorting Jojo to "Get Back" to his home in Tucson, Arizona, in the 1969 hit song, the Beatles' Paul McCartney and his wife, Linda, purchased 150 acres of ranchland (pictured) on the outskirts of the city, where they could relax and ride horses with their children.

PAUL MCCARTNEY RANCH

WHAT A Beatle's second home

WHERE South of E. Redington Rd. around Mile Two (behind Tanque Verde Ranch)

COST Free

PRO TIP While the McCartney ranch (which Paul still owns) has a locked gate, it can be viewed from a distance.

Yoko Ono. Or maybe the lyrics didn't mean any of those things. What is certain is that "Get Back" proved to be the final song on the last album the band ever recorded—and Tucson is indelibly memorialized in it.

48 PEARL HARBOR PATHWAY

Which ship is honored with an often overlooked tribute on the UA campus?

When the Japanese bombed Pearl Harbor in December 1941, 1,177 sailors and Marines—including eight from Arizona and one, James Van Horn, a seventeen-year-old seaman from Tucson—were killed aboard the aircraft carrier USS *Arizona*, whose sinking triggered U.S. entry into World War II. In 2016, on the seventy-fifth anniversary of the bombing, the University of Arizona dedicated a memorial to those who perished, situated on the grassy pedestrian mall that forms the center of campus.

The most visible part of the memorial consists of panels that display brass medallions commemorating the name, rank, and home state of each victim. But unless you know what you're looking for, it's easy to miss a far less prominent but still noteworthy part of the memorial: an exact full-scale 597-foot-long, 97-foot-wide outline of the ship's deck. Marked by a dark red rubberized track that's almost obscured by the mall's lush grass, it's fair to say that most UA visitors have no idea it's there.

USS *ARIZONA* MEMORIAL

WHAT A tribute to Pearl Harbor victims

WHERE 1200 E. University Blvd.

COST Free

PRO TIP The campus mall is a showplace of desert vegetation and makes for a pleasant walk.

The flagpole of the memorial is aligned with the tower of UA's student union, which contains a bell salvaged from the ship.

The University of Arizona's memorial to the USS Arizona, *which was sunk at Pearl Harbor in 1941, features both commemorative medallions of victims and an easy-to-overlook 597-foot-long outline of the ship's deck, marked by a rubberized track partially obscured by lush grass.*

To follow the entire outline of the ship, start just before the steps on the east side of the beautifully restored Old Main, the oldest building on the UA campus, which served as the base for the Naval Training School during the war. At this point, the path is marked by red bricks for several yards until it continues into the grass. The rubberized track then leads to the part of the memorial with the commemorative medallions, before continuing the path that marks the remainder of the deck, eventually leading back to Old Main. The entire length of the *Arizona*'s outline can be comfortably walked in ten minutes or so, not counting any time spent perusing the commemorative plaques.

49 A CHRISTMASTIME TREAT

Where can you find the Southwest's largest nativity scene?

From November to March, visitors to the Tucson Museum of Art can enjoy a bonus included in the price of admission: a special treasure that's located within the museum's "historic block" of nineteenth-century adobe buildings. That treasure is called *El Nacimiento*, an extravagant eight-hundred-piece nativity scene that fills an entire room inside La Casa Cordova, thought to be Tucson's oldest surviving residence. Depicting the story of Christmas as well as other biblical tales, it's the handiwork of Tucson resident Maria Luisa Leon Teña, who spent more than thirty years—from 1977 to 2009—building and refining it. For much of that time, she re-created and updated the intricate exhibit each year, meticulously cleaning the figures and making any necessary repairs. Now safely displayed behind glass, *El Nacimiento* ranks as the Southwest's largest and longest-running work of its kind.

Listed on the National Register of Historic Places, La Casa Cordova was originally located within the walled Presidio, Tucson's first residential area (most of the walls were torn down in the 1850s). Named for the Cordova family who lived there from 1944 to 1973, the home may have predated the 1854 Gadsden Purchase, through which the United States acquired much of southern Arizona from Mexico. Some historians believe it may date from as early as 1848, when Tucson was still part of the Mexican state of Sonora.

EL NACIMIENTO

WHAT An eight-hundred-piece nativity scene

WHERE 140 N. Main Ave.

COST $10 (for Museum of Art)

PRO TIP The museum is free for Tucson residents each Thursday from 5 to 8 p.m.

El Nacimiento, *an 800-piece nativity scene, fills an entire room inside La Casa Cordova at the Tucson Museum of Art. The exhibit, created over thirty years by Tucson resident Maria Luisa Leon Teña, is open annually from November to March.*

El Nacimiento was constructed in honor of Teña's late mother, well known for creating her own elaborate nativity scenes—a popular art form honed in Mexico over many generations.

50

LIVING LABORATORY

Why is this Tucson hill called the birthplace of ecology?

Tumamoc Hill, best known for offering challenging and scenic cardio workouts for the thousands of Tucson hikers who tackle its steep eight-hundred-foot elevation rise each year, has a separate distinction to which most climbers may never have given a second thought. While signs note that Tumamoc is used as a University of Arizona research facility and hikers are asked to stay away from forbidden areas, the nature of that research goes largely unnoticed.

Well over a century ago, in 1903, scientists established the Carnegie Institution's Desert Botanical Laboratory on Tumamoc with the intent of studying how Sonoran Desert plants adapt to their hot, arid environments. Botanist Volney Spalding laid out hillside plots that represented differing habitats and plants and then mapped and photographed each piece of vegetation within them, from the tallest saguaro cacti to the most fragile wildflowers. That work has gone on ever since, taken over by the U.S. Forest Service in 1940 and, since 1956, by the University of Arizona. Tumamoc's 860-acre Desert Laboratory is now the site of the world's longest continuously monitored vegetation plots and is therefore considered the birthplace of modern ecology. Tumamoc has also been a subject of study in the fields of archaeology, astronomy, and history (the area is thought to be the oldest continuously

A free mobile app ("The Tumamoc Tour") tells the story of Sonoran Desert ecology for those who climb and descend Tumamoc, timed to an average walking pace.

Best known for the challenging hike to its summit, steep Tumamoc Hill is also home to a landmark University of Arizona botanical research facility that has earned it the moniker of "birthplace of modern ecology."

inhabited locale in the United States, dating back 4,100 years). It's all part of this living laboratory's delicate balancing act between preservation and recreation, science and sport— and after more than 115 years, it's managing it all quite well.

DESERT LABORATORY ON TUMAMOC HILL

WHAT The birthplace of modern ecology

WHERE W. Anklam Rd. and Tumamoc Hill Rd.

COST Free

PRO TIP Tumamoc is open for climbing from 4 a.m. to 10 p.m. daily.

51

UNSUNG LANDMARK

What's the story behind that old water tower on Broadway?

Rising just off the busy Broadway Boulevard corridor southwest of the corner of Randolph Way and partially obscured by

> ## EL CONQUISTADOR WATER TOWER
>
> **WHAT** A landmark water tower
>
> **WHERE** Broadway Blvd. and Randolph Way
>
> **COST** Free
>
> **PRO TIP** Best viewing is just down Randolph Way.

surrounding buildings and trees, the almost century-old El Conquistador Water Tower has at times come perilously close to destruction. It hasn't stored any water since the middle of the last century. Yet the Spanish Colonial Revival structure has managed to emerge as a protected historic structure and will now stand as long as its steel legs will hold it.

But that's only part of its somewhat convoluted history. Erected in 1928, the same year as the legendary El Conquistador Hotel across Broadway, the water tower was popularly thought to have been built to supply the hotel, but no evidence of piping there has been found. Instead, it served the residents of the then-new and highly upscale Colonia Solana neighborhood, which it adjoins. And unlike the rather exotic seventy-room hotel, known for its glamorous Hollywood guests but bankrupt by 1935 and torn down in 1968 to make way for a shopping mall, it's the water tower that continues the proud El Conquistador name.

Built by developer John W. Murphey, the tower was spiffed up four years later by the noted local architect Roy Place, who added a stucco facade, a tile roof, and a cast-iron weather vane depicting a miner with his donkey. But when

The El Conquistador Water Tower in midtown Tucson, constructed the same year (1928) as the legendary but long-defunct El Conquistador Hotel, has managed to survive perching pigeons, complaining neighbors, and decades of disuse to gain new respect as a city landmark.

the El Conquistador Hotel was demolished, the local pigeons needed a new perch and chose the water tower, upsetting some neighbors who convinced the cash-strapped city that the by-then-obsolete tower needed to go. This in turn upset other neighbors and historical preservationists, who prevailed after a series of battles. The tower was restored by the city in 1994, when it was honored as one of just six official Tucson landmarks.

The El Conquistador Hotel has long since been replaced by the less-glamorous El Con shopping mall, which includes a multiscreen cinema, a Walmart, and several surrounding fast-casual food places.

<u>52</u> GOING PEACEFULLY POSTAL

Where can you find a real 1890s post office in Tucson?

Tucked away on a side street just west of the University of Arizona campus, the Postal History Foundation opens a window into the world of philately (stamp collecting). Collectors, or any history buffs, should enjoy the exhibits of old-time postal equipment. Dedicated philatelists can peruse stamps for sale or immerse themselves in the adjacent research library. And even those who've done no more than fix stamps to envelopes can discover how the foundation reaches out to schools and teachers for lessons and field trips through the medium of stamps.

Chances are that when you walk in you'll be greeted by one of the volunteers—mostly retirees who are also stamp aficionados—who will guide you through the centerpiece of the little museum, a circa-1890 post office brought here from Naco, Arizona, near the Mexican border, featuring a wall of solid-brass post office boxes dating from pre-home-delivery days. Within the tiny former post office are some intriguing items out of postal history, including antique hand-run cancellation machines, one so rare that the Smithsonian Institution has its eyes on it, and three-cent-stamp-dispensing machines (which really was the price of a first-class stamp as late as 1958).

After the tour, you'll receive sample materials that include little packages of (used) stamps—perhaps inspiring youngsters you know to start their own collections.

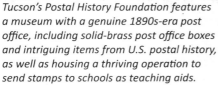

Tucson's Postal History Foundation features a museum with a genuine 1890s-era post office, including solid-brass post office boxes and intriguing items from U.S. postal history, as well as housing a thriving operation to send stamps to schools as teaching aids.

Be sure to check out other rooms where volunteers sort through huge piles of stamps from around the globe to send to schools around the country. Teachers may request U.S. stamps that honor national symbols, for example, or various themes such as animals or sports from countries around the globe. The foundation then sends out packets of stamps, worksheets and other educational materials appropriate to the themes. Meanwhile, local students can visit on field trips that introduce them to the museum or even encourage them to design their own stamps honoring Tucson's heritage.

POSTAL HISTORY FOUNDATION

WHAT A haven for philatelists

WHERE 920 N.1st Ave.

COST Free

PRO TIP Stamp collection donations are welcomed.

LOST BARRIO FIND

Where's the best place to stock up on Italian foods in Tucson?

In a city where Mexican food is king, Italian food (beyond pizza) can get short shrift. Enter Roma Imports, an Italian deli-restaurant tucked into the far reaches of the Barrio San Antonio (also known as the Lost Barrio because it's cut off from most of the rest of the city by two freeways). Even if you can find the Lost Barrio, you'd be highly unlikely to stumble upon Roma Imports by accident. Except for the red, green, and white awning and flag out front, there's little indication that Tucson's best Italian food purveyor resides among the mix of nearby small warehouses, light manufacturing plants, and modest residences.

After twenty years in business, though, Roma Imports has survived mainly on word-of-mouth (and indeed, mouth-watering) praise from well-fed customers. Roma serves up Italian food in three ways. Up front is a well-stocked and tantalizing deli section, including a wide selection of dry pastas, antipasti, imported olive oils, specialty cheeses, and refrigerators and freezers filled with sausages, ready-to-cook lasagnas and raviolis, sauces, and desserts, most made on the premises. In the rear is a casual but colorfully decorated restaurant, especially popular at lunchtime, with a menu focusing on hot and cold deli sandwiches. Roma will also arrange impressive platters of antipasti for catering parties and gatherings.

ROMA IMPORTS

WHAT "Hidden" Italian deli-restaurant

WHERE 627 S. Vine Ave.

COST Varies with purchase; reasonable prices

PRO TIP Roma offers vegetarian, organic, and gluten-free options.

Roma Imports is located deep in Tucson's Lost Barrio, but Italian-food aficionados still make their way there for the city's top selection of pastas, antipasti, imported olive oils, specialty cheeses, and freezers filled with ready-to-cook lasagnas and raviolis.

Perhaps surprisingly, long-time owner Lilian Spieth was born in Calcutta, India, and has also lived in Israel and Europe; watch for some of her international dishes among the frozen foods.

54 NOT YOUR AVERAGE SELFIE

Where can you find the archives of Ansel Adams and other master photographers?

Founded by Ansel Adams and four other master photographers in 1975, the University of Arizona's Center for Creative Photography is a remarkable repository of fine-art-quality photographs, having amassed more than ninety thousand works by some 2,200 photographers. One of the largest such collections in the world, it includes all of Ansel Adams' negatives and 456 works by Richard Avedon. Along with Adams and his four cofounders—Wynn Bullock, Harry Callahan, Aaron Siskind, and Frederick Sommer—more than 260 of the finest photographers of the twentieth century have donated their entire archival works to the center, which moved to its current location in the campus's Fine Arts Complex in 1989.

The center draws on its archives to display special exhibitions in its spacious first-floor galleries. Recently, for instance, it featured a stunning selection of portraits by Avedon and landscapes by Adams, with a number of images famous in their own right. The exhibitions each continue for several months and number two to three per year. These are always free of charge and open to the public.

The university's pedestrian-only Fine Arts Complex is also home to the UA Museum of Art and to six-hundred-seat Crowder Hall, which presents guest concerts.

At the University of Arizona's Center for Creative Photography, you can view special exhibitions of fine art photos by the likes of Ansel Adams and Richard Avedon. Adams donated his entire archives to the Center, which he helped found in 1975.

The center is also a tremendous resource for anyone interested in the history of photography dating back to the nineteenth century, with special strength in twentieth-century North American artists. Scholars,

CENTER FOR CREATIVE PHOTOGRAPHY

WHAT Repository of fine-art photography

WHERE 1030 N. Olive Rd.

COST Free

PRO TIP Park at the convenient Park Avenue Garage at the corner of Speedway and Park.

authors, students, and others can access a wealth of materials, ranging from rare books to journals, oral histories, and exhibition catalogues. Altogether the center preserves more than eight million archival objects. Special events include lectures, book signings, and film screenings.

55 THE GAMES PEOPLE PLAYED

Where can you find ruins of ancient Indian ballcourts?

Among the most intriguing archaeological finds in the Tucson area are dwellings and other artifacts of the prehistoric Hohokam people, who inhabited the region for at least a millennium from around 500 AD to 1500 AD. And some of the most fascinating findings have been the ruins of ballcourts similar to those found at ancient Mayan sites in Mexico and Central America.

HOHOKAM BALLCOURT

WHAT Ancient Native American Ruins

WHERE 1570 N. Oracle Rd. (Arizona State Route 77)

COST $7 per car

PRO TIP Rangers lead periodic tours to the site.

The courts, used for ballgames and found at large Hohokam villages, are sunken oval-shaped fields lined by earthen berms or piled rocks, where spectators could sit and cheer well above the action; game balls were fashioned from plant sap. In Mexico, the ballcourts were associated with ritual sacrifice; speculation is that the losing team captain (or perhaps even the winning one!) forfeited his life. But with the Hohokam, it's thought that the games were a way of bonding and reducing tensions between villages.

Following winter and spring rains especially, you may encounter running water in the washes leading to the trail; most hikers remove their shoes and socks to cross.

Not far from the entrance to Catalina State Park north of Tucson, the often-overlooked Romero Ruins Interpretive Trail leads to archaeological finds such as traces of an ancient Hohokam tribal ballcourt similar to that seen in Mayan ruins of Mexico.

The most accessible of a handful of ballcourts that archaeologists have discovered in the Tucson area is at Catalina State Park north of the city. Not far from the park entrance, the often-overlooked Romero Ruins Interpretive Trail forms a three-quarter-mile loop around the remnants of an ancient Hohokam pit house village built atop a crest with magnificent views of the Catalina Mountains.

The existence of the ballcourt is one reason some experts think this village—with a population of up to three hundred residents—may have been a Hohokam cultural or religious center. (Watch for the marker, as the remnants of the eighty-foot-long ballcourt are easily missed.) Along the trail you can also view excavated fragments of the Hohokams' village walls, as well as the much later stone ruins of nineteenth-century pioneer rancher Francisco Romero's settlement.

56

BIRDING BONANZA

Where might you spot chestnut-sided warblers and groove-billed anis?

Originally built in 1996 as a water treatment facility, Sweetwater Wetlands is an off-the-beaten-path urban oasis and wildlife habitat in northwest Tucson, featuring trails that wind past ponds surrounded by thick stands of cattails as well as willows, cottonwoods, and saltbush. The combination of water and vegetation has attracted numerous species of birds—including wrens, blackbirds, warblers, song sparrows, Abert's towhees, and waterfowl—and in turn the birds have attracted a steady stream of local birders, binoculars in hand.

The birders have been rewarded by some rare sightings over the years, including least grebes, chestnut-sided warblers, and groove-billed anis, among others. For a desert community, Tucson attracts an unexpectedly diverse bird population, thanks to its variety of elevations, welcoming climate, and location along migratory flyways, while Southeastern Arizona in general is known as one of the top birding sites in the country.

Non-birders, especially youngsters, may be equally enchanted by the ducks, egrets, and other waterfowl inhabiting the ponds. A deck with gazebo along the paved main trail is a popular spot for visitors to gaze out over the water, while various unpaved trails lead to more wetlands. It all makes Sweetwater a surprisingly peaceful retreat just around the corner from an area of light industrial warehouses and small businesses not far from Interstate 10.

SWEETWATER WETLANDS

WHAT An urban birding sanctuary

WHERE Sweetwater Dr.

COST Free

PRO TIP The ponds are drained for a few weeks in late winter for annual drying and maintenance in February through mid-March.

Sweetwater Wetlands, hidden away among office buildings and warehouses near Interstate 10, is a quiet spot to observe birds attracted to its ponds, streams, trees, and rich vegetation. Trails lead to observation decks and gazebos overlooking the ponds.

The Wings Over Willcox festival each January in Willcox, east of Tucson along I-10, celebrates the arrival of giant sandhill cranes during their colorful winter migration.

57

A FUTURISTIC FLOP

What current research facility was home to a bizarre 1990s scientific experiment?

Today, Biosphere 2 is a scientific research facility devoted to studying worldwide ecosystems, from rainforests to deserts, oceans to swamps. About twenty-four miles north of Tucson, it's run by the University of Arizona and is open to the public for tours. But back in the early 1990s, it was a controversial—bordering on the bizarre—privately funded $150-million-dollar experiment to see if humans could survive in a man-made, sealed environment for two years while growing all their own food; recycling all their air, water, and waste; and maintaining all other aspects of self-sufficiency. The rounded glass and steel module, which seemed straight out of science fiction, would be pollution free and, its backers dreamed, lead to similar colonies around the globe and even on other planets.

In September 1991, eight "Biospherians"—four men and four women, mostly Americans—donned blue jumpsuits and, with much fanfare, were locked into the facility, which also harbored 3,800 plant and animal species, a coral reef, and a mangrove swamp. But the experiment didn't go exactly as planned. Oxygen had to be pumped in after oxygen-eating bacteria dangerously lowered the supply inside. Needed supplies ranging from vitamins to mouse traps were surreptitiously delivered, a total of twenty-nine times in all. Food was difficult to grow under cloudy conditions the first several months. Pests proliferated.

BIOSPHERE 2

WHAT Scientific facility with a bizarre past

WHERE 32540 S. Biosphere Rd., Oracle

COST Adults, $20; ages 6–12, $13

PRO TIP Biosphere 2 tours last one and one-quarter hours.

While the futuristic Biosphere 2 north of Tucson is now a successful University of Arizona research facility, it started out as a bizarre privately funded scientific experiment to determine if people could live in a completely self-sufficient, sealed, man-made environment. It failed.

While the eight eventually emerged in good health, though looking much thinner and paler, Biosphere 2 was ridiculed by many scientists as a monumental waste of resources. The company financing the project, Space Biospheres Ventures, took a financial beating and its leadership was fired. Shortly after a second crew of Biospherians began their own stint inside in 1994, two of the initial crewmembers—who said they feared for the new crew's safety—vandalized their former home and ended the dream.

One-time Trump administration advisor Steve Bannon, then an investment banker, helped orchestrate the firings of Biosphere 2's officers in April 1994.

⁵⁸ PLAYING PIONEER

Was that a cannon shot I just heard?

Passersby within earshot of the Presidio Museum, a reconstructed version of the 1775 original Tucson Presidio, or fort, where the city was born, may be surprised to hear the periodic sounds of cannon fire erupting on occasional Saturdays. Not to worry—the Redcoats aren't attacking. It's simply a Living History Days presentation at the museum, when volunteers play the parts of residents from Tucson's earliest days, starting with the colorfully costumed Spanish soldiers who demonstrate military drills and dramatic hourly firings of a replica cannon. Also on hand to entertain and instruct are blacksmiths, weavers, candlemakers, and merchants wearing period dress from the late 1700s and early 1800s.

Emphasis is on interactive activities. Attendees can try their hands at pumping the bellows of the blacksmith's forge, spinning cotton, or grinding corn. They can also learn how muskets were fired, sample handmade tortillas and fresh-baked bread, and play children's games of the era. (Families are drawn to Living History Days so parents can give their kids a look at what life was like before cell phones, Netflix, Instagram—and even texting, if you can imagine it.) Along with the standard demonstrations, each Living History Day has a special theme, such as Arizona history, the diversity of cultures in Tucson, and

LIVING HISTORY DAYS AT THE PRESIDIO MUSEUM

WHAT A chance to relive Tucson's earliest days

WHERE 196 N. Court Ave.

COST $5

PRO TIP Living History Days are staged October through April, 10 a.m. to 3 p.m., on the second Saturday of each month.

Demonstrations of eighteenth-century musket drills, blacksmithing, cannon firing, weaving, and other early Tucson pioneer skills are on display at the Presidio Museum's monthly Living History Days presentations, staged by volunteers in period dress.

gardening and foods, so there's always something new to see. Or should we say something old to see? Living History Days shows there's still a lot we can learn from Tucson's earliest settlers.

On non-Living History Days, the Presidio Museum is still well worth a visit, showcasing an authentic two-thousand-year-old Native American pit house, an 1860s Sonoran row house, and the Presidio wall.

59 COLOSSAL HIDEOUT

Is the loot from two train robberies still stashed in a cave?

Since Kartchner Caverns opened to the public in 1999, the Tucson region's other major cave complex, Colossal Cave Mountain Park, has played second fiddle to its spectacular cousin. But because it has a long documented history— artifacts have been discovered dating from prehistoric times— Colossal Cave has some tales to tell. (Well, at least its guides do—the cave itself isn't talking.) While there are plenty of colorful variations on legends of train robbers holing up in the cave back in the 1880s, the "official" version of the account is that in 1887 a gang of masked bandits hid out there after ambushing two trains and stealing thousands of dollars in cash and gold.

Their M.O.: setting off explosives on the tracks and riddling the cars with bullets to halt the trains. After the second robbery, they rode off into the Rincon Mountains with their

COLOSSAL CAVE MOUNTAIN PARK

WHAT Colorful cave with colorful past

WHERE 16721 E. Old Spanish Trail, Vail

COST Adults, $18; ages 5–12, $9

PRO TIP Tours run every hour from 8 a.m. to 5 p.m. daily.

The park, located twenty-two miles east of Tucson, also contains hiking and biking trails, which anyone can use for free.

Legends of 1887 bandits and train robberies still reverberate through the walls of Colossal Cave east of Tucson. Stolen money and gold from the robberies were never recovered, and speculation is that the loot may have been hidden among the cave's still unexplored nether regions.

haul, and posses tracked them to the site of Five-Mile Cave at Mountain Springs, now known as Colossal Cave. Apparently already familiar with the rugged underground terrain, the bandits were able to successfully hide there and escape. The money and gold were never recovered, and rumors have it that stolen loot may still be hidden somewhere in the cave's nether regions; only a few miles of an estimated forty miles of natural passageways have been fully explored.

Colossal Cave is dry, meaning that its star attractions— stalactites, stalagmites, columns, and draperies—are no longer forming. Inside, temperatures are a pleasant seventy degrees year-round. The fifty-minute, half-mile-long guided tours require climbing down six and a half stories (363 stair steps) and then climbing back up.

CELEBRITY REHAB

Where do the stars go to treat their addictions?

Maybe it's the desert air, maybe it's the reputation of the facilities, maybe it's the private, secluded settings, but something draws celebrities to seek treatment at Tucson's rehab clinics. And the area rehab center that seems to attract the most Hollywood stars, musicians, athletes, and other celebs who are trying to overcome various types of addictions is Sierra Tucson.

Situated on 160 acres with gorgeous up-close views of the Catalina Mountains about thirty miles north of downtown, the upscale Sierra Tucson has been treating alcohol and drug addictions as well as eating and mood disorders and other mental health issues for more than thirty-five years. Along the way, such well-known figures as Robert Downey Jr., Tiger Woods, Rob Lowe, Ringo Starr, Michael Douglas, Martin Lawrence, and Patrick Swayze are all reported to have been treated there. (While Sierra Tucson promises "the highest level of confidentiality," celebrity rehab stints have a way of becoming public.)

Billing itself as a place of "peace, hope, and healing" while "connecting the mind, body, and spirit," Sierra Tucson offers an integrative treatment program that melds counseling sessions and psychiatry with alternative approaches such as acupuncture and yoga. Recreational facilities include a swimming pool, walking paths, a rock climbing wall, a gym, stables, a ropes course, and a chance to visit with therapeutic dogs and Sheldon the Therapy Tortoise. The clinic's semiprivate rooms each contain two beds and private baths, but chances are if you seek treatment there, you won't find yourself sleeping next to a celebrity—he or she could presumably afford to pay for the whole room.

Walking the labyrinth at Sierra Tucson, a rehab facility north of Tucson, is one of many recreational and spiritually related activities available to those (including a number of celebrities) who seek treatments for various addictions there.

SIERRA TUCSON

WHAT An addiction rehab facility

WHERE 39580 S. Lago del Oro Pkwy.

COST $1,300 per day per room

PRO TIP For information on treatments, call 844-335-1495.

Rolling Stones guitarist Ron Wood is reported to have once checked into another upscale rehab center in the area, Cottonwood Tucson, which emphasizes its "spiritual path" to recovery.

61 IN SEARCH OF CRESTED SAGUAROS

What causes these "beautiful freaks of nature"?

Saguaro cacti, the "Sentinels of the Desert" that are an iconic symbol of Tucson, are plentiful both within and near the city. Best known for their multiple "arms," which give them a variety of shapes and first appear when they're about fifty years old, saguaros can live for up to two centuries. Occasionally, though, the cacti also grow a kind of fan-like headdress or crown at the tips of their main stem. Called crested (or cristate) saguaros, these cacti are so rare—just one out of every ten thousand—that only a few dozen have been found in Tucson's Saguaro National Park, home to thousands of saguaros of every size and description. Local explorer Bob Cardell, who spent decades tracking down more than 2,200 crested saguaros throughout Arizona's Sonora Desert, has called them "beautiful freaks of nature."

No one knows exactly what creates a crested saguaro—theories range from frost damage and lightning strikes to insect infestations and genetic mutations—but count yourself fortunate if you are able to spot even one in the wild. You don't need to spend hours or days, though, tromping through the desert like Cardell. Instead, make your way to the Old Main building on the University of Arizona campus mall, which has an easily accessible example nearby. (Alternatively, you can walk the south loop trail at Tohono Chul Park—$13 admission; tohonochul.org—and keep a sharp eye out for the crested saguaro there.)

About one in ten thousand Saguaro cacti—an iconic symbol of Tucson—are crested, growing a fan-like crown atop their main stems. In the city, you can see examples of these rare cacti on the University of Arizona campus and at Tohono Chul gardens.

CRESTED SAGUARO

WHAT A rare cactus mutation

WHERE Old Main, 1200 E. University Blvd.

COST Free

PRO TIP Look for the crested saguaro on the northeast corner of UA's Old Main.

The Crested Saguaro Society (crestedsaguarosociety.org) is dedicated to locating and cataloguing these rare specimens in their natural settings.

62

SNAKING AROUND

Why did the 280-foot-long diamondback cross the road?

Motorists cruising down Broadway Boulevard just east of downtown may feel oddly reptilian as they pass beneath a 280-foot-long pedestrian bridge fashioned to resemble a giant diamondback rattlesnake. Built as a public art project in 2002, it's the prizewinning design of local artist Simon Donovan, who wanted to pay homage to one of the desert's iconic creatures while offering pedestrians and cyclists a safe and handy way to cross six lanes of traffic below. The metal mesh exterior is designed and decorated in anatomically correct snake detail. The Federal Highway Administration once named it one of the top road projects in the United States.

To fully appreciate Donovan's vision, though, you need to walk or bike through the belly of the diamondback, which provides a covered link from the southeastern side of the city to the northern. From one end you enter into the snake's open mouth below its fearsome fangs and eyes. From the other end

RATTLESNAKE BRIDGE

WHAT A bridge resembling a rattler

WHERE Broadway Blvd. and Euclid St.

COST Free

PRO TIP Real rattlesnakes inhabit parts of Tucson, but they're as leery of you as you are of them.

Nearby, the 240-foot-long, 14-foot-wide Basket Bridge—with a Tohono O'odham woven basket design—crosses over Park Avenue and allows cyclists a safe link between southeast Tucson and downtown.

A bridge shaped like a rattlesnake is Tucson's most distinctive pedestrian crossing, offering walkers and cyclists a safe passage over busy Broadway Boulevard while entertaining them a bit as well. Whether you enter through the tail or the mouth of the rattler, you won't forget the experience.

you exit past a thirty-foot-long tail rattle that extends straight up into the air.

Some of the original bells and whistles that accompanied the Rattlesnake Bridge have at least temporarily been dismantled due to maintenance cutbacks. Formerly, when a pedestrian or bicycle would enter the bridge, a motion sensor would set off speakers emitting a loud rattling sound, a phenomenon guaranteed to draw shrieks from young children (and from some unsuspecting adults). The snake's eyes once glowed as well. But even without these special effects, the Rattlesnake Bridge is an "only in Tucson" example of public art at its zaniest.

63

THE WISHING SHRINE

How did a shrine to a sinner become a cultural landmark?

Set back from the street in a nondescript lot, it's easy to overlook El Tiradito—also known as the Wishing Shrine—in Barrio Viejo. And it's safe to say that thousands of annual visitors to the Tucson Convention Center just to the north are unaware of its existence. But the shrine, listed on the National Register of Historic Places, is a poignant symbol of Tucson's Hispanic Catholic traditions and folk customs and has survived decades of upheaval in the city's oldest remaining neighborhood.

The legend of El Tiradito (The Castaway or Fallen One) tells of an amorous ranch worker, Juan Oliveros, who was caught by his father-in-law in the warm embrace of . . . his mother-in-law. Oliveros is said to have been slain or committed suicide and was then buried on the spot, which is a few blocks from the shrine's current location (it was moved nearly a century ago during street repairs). Spontaneous written prayers and offerings for Juan soon appeared at the site—wishes both for him and, increasingly, for those leaving the offerings. It's said that if you light a candle there and it burns through the night, your wish will be granted, and enough wishes have apparently come true that the shrine's reputation for answered prayers has grown and flourished since 1870. While it's unusual for a Catholic shrine to honor an unconsecrated sinner, that only adds to its mystique.

By 1971, the shrine had attained such cultural significance that its existence helped stop construction of a freeway threatening to cut through the heart of Barrio Viejo.

Flowers, candles, and written prayers and wishes surround El Tiradito, also known as the Wishing Shrine. The shrine marks the death of the victim of a romance gone wrong 150 years ago, but legend has it that prayers will be answered if you burn a candle there.

El Tiradito's dominant feature is a twelve-foot-high, U-shaped adobe wall with a seven-foot-high niche in the center. Offerings are abundant within the niche and surroundings, with a jumble of written prayers and messages, candles, photographs, and flowers making for a lively tableau. It's thought to be the only shrine of its kind still extant north of the Mexican border, and it was restored by the city in 2010.

\underline{64} A QUIRKY ROYAL MANSE

Is that a real castle up on the hill?

Crowning a hilltop in southwest Tucson, Mollohan Castle comes complete with all the requisite castle parts: crenellated roofs, a turret, a dungeon, stone floors, decorative swords, and a retractable drawbridge complete with moat. It doesn't come with a lot of history, but not all castles have to be old. Dating from the late 1980s, Mollohan Castle was built as a kind of fantasy retreat by the late Pat Bruno, in honor of his parents, "King Richard and Queen Frances of Bruno." While working on it, he survived mostly on white bread and baloney sandwiches, along with lots of aspirin to ease the pain from moving heavy construction materials himself.

The quirky castle is now owned by Daniel Reese, who bought it in 1996 and has been operating it as a vacation rental for several years, even while continuing to "smooth out its rough edges" and add to its features. Reese has installed some spiral stairs and recently finished the moat. He lives in a lower-level apartment in the castle.

The castle, which sleeps up to eight guests, features a bedroom in the tower and one in the medieval dungeon as well, though you may not want to banish any over-imaginative kids down there. It's reached through a trapdoor in the kitchen. There are plenty of twenty-first-century amenities, though, including a kitchen, air conditioning, heating, Wi-Fi, and a pool table on the deck. And it offers some terrific 360-degree views looking out over the city—some might say fit for royalty.

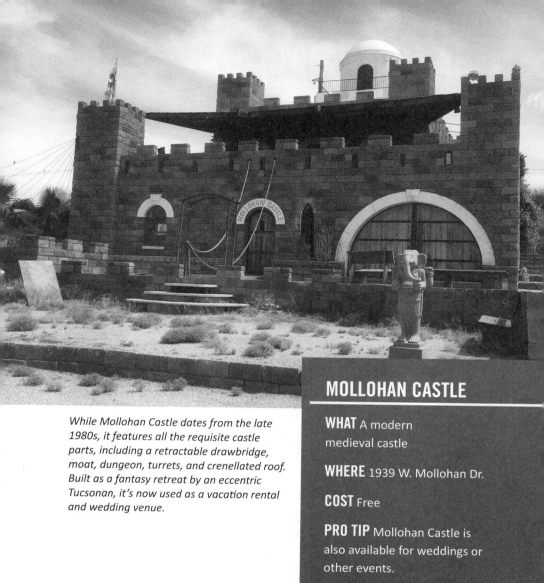

While Mollohan Castle dates from the late 1980s, it features all the requisite castle parts, including a retractable drawbridge, moat, dungeon, turrets, and crenellated roof. Built as a fantasy retreat by an eccentric Tucsonan, it's now used as a vacation rental and wedding venue.

MOLLOHAN CASTLE

WHAT A modern medieval castle

WHERE 1939 W. Mollohan Dr.

COST Free

PRO TIP Mollohan Castle is also available for weddings or other events.

From the castle you can access miles of trails in Tucson Mountain Park or head out to the Arizona-Sonora Desert Museum, Saguaro National Park, or Old Tucson.

SEEDS OF LIFE

Where can you find seeds for growing desert gardens?

Native Seeds/SEARCH took root more than thirty-five years ago when its founders sat down with Tohono O'odham tribal elders and asked what their indigenous communities needed to create sustainable gardens in the water-starved deserts. The answer: "The seeds for the foods our grandparents used to grow."

Today, Native Seeds preserves ninety heritage seed species and some 1,900 accessions—a particular seed variety grown by one farmer—in its Tucson cold-storage seed bank. The seeds come from a desert area roughly stretching from Las Vegas, Nevada, to Las Vegas, New Mexico, and from Durango, Colorado, to Durango, Mexico (with Tucson falling right in the middle). Many of the seed varieties are rare or endangered. Also preserved are a number of wild ancestors of domesticated plants.

Many seed crops, though, are grown in abundance and sold at Native Seeds' beautifully organized retail store, located separately from the seed bank. There you will find rack upon rack of neatly packaged seed packets (all assembled by volunteers) containing the makings of a potential desert garden or landscape: many varieties of chile seeds, green vegetable seeds, bean seeds, corn seeds, gourd seeds, squash seeds, herb seeds, melon seeds, tomato seeds, sunflower seeds, desert wildflower seeds . . . the list goes on. All seeds

---

Consider the nutritious, endemic tepary bean—a trendy item in many Tucson restaurants—for your next meal. You can buy them at Native Seeds in either seed or ready-to-cook form.

The Native Seeds/SEARCH retail store is stocked with racks of seed packets containing the makings of a potential desert garden or landscape, as well as edibles such as bags of tepary beans, mesquite flour, and toasted barrel cactus seeds.

are organic, open pollinated, and non-GMO.

The store also sells related products such as mesquite flour, toasted barrel cactus seeds, chiltepin chile-infused water, and traditional herbal pain remedies. You can also visit the separate Native Seeds Conservation Center, where the seed bank and gardens are located, for tours, classes, workshops, and volunteer opportunities.

NATIVE SEEDS/ SEARCH

WHAT A desert seed shop

WHERE 3061 N. Campbell Ave. (retail store)

COST $3.25 to $4.95 for seed packets

PRO TIP Call 520-622-0830 before visiting the Conservation Center.

66 A SLICE OF THE MIDWEST

Why is there a neighborhood of green lawns in Tucson?

What happens when you try to transplant a slice of the Midwest onto a Southwestern desert city? You get Winterhaven, one of the most controversial of Tucson's historic neighborhoods. Winterhaven was the brainchild of developer C. B. Richards, who built it from 1949 to 1961—and introduced the concept of grassy lawns and non-native pine trees into a city where desert plants and landscaping form the vast majority of residents' yards. For many Tucsonans, Winterhaven evokes the image of that rival (and often disdained) metropolis to the north, Phoenix, where grassy lawns can be found in abundance. Winterhaven's nod to its Midwestern roots continues in its wide winding streets and ranch-style homes, many designed by a prominent local architect of the day, Anne Jackson Rysdale. The neighborhood is self-contained and it's easy to drive past it without ever knowing it's there.

WINTERHAVEN

WHAT A Midwestern-style neighborhood

WHERE Bounded by Ft. Lowell, Prince, and Country Club Rds. and Tucson Blvd.

COST Free

PRO TIP Bring Food Bank donations for the Festival of Lights.

There is no non-resident parking available inside Winterhaven during the Festival of Lights, and the only drive-through night is December 26. But you can reserve trolleys, hayrides, and party bikes.

The Winterhaven neighborhood is known for its grassy lawns—unusual in Tucson—and its annual winter Festival of Lights, when many residents turn their houses and yards into illuminated winter wonderlands. This house (pictured) undoubtedly belongs to unabashed Arizona Wildcats fans.

Perhaps as penance for its imported Midwestern ways—or perhaps merely reflecting them—Winterhaven has staged a dazzling annual Festival of Lights at Christmastime ever since 1949, initiated by C. B. Richards himself. For two weeks in December, most neighborhood houses are adorned with elaborate lighting displays and lawn decorations that draw steady crowds of pedestrians after dark. So, somewhat ironically, many Tucsonans never actually get a glimpse of Winterhaven, and its grassy lawns that originally brought it prominence, in the light of day.

67

A WALLED OASIS

Where can you enjoy vegetarian food and a peacock too?

Located on a side street just a short distance off busy North First Avenue, Govinda's is like a welcoming oasis in the middle of Tucson. A gateway in the walled enclave leads to a spacious and airy outdoor dining patio with a central splashing fountain and towering palms. Tables are equipped with large umbrellas to shade the sun, while diners feast on well-prepared vegetarian and vegan dishes, many with Indian accents, served buffet-style. All-you-can-eat vegetables, grains, fruits, bean dishes, and do-it-yourself salads all sparkle here and can appeal to omnivores as well as non-meat eaters. Indoor seating is also available, but the patio area—where the walls are lined with colorful mandalas—is the big draw in nice weather. Indian music plays softly in the background.

After your meal, be sure to check out the aviary to the rear of the restaurant, inhabited by a magnificently plumed peacock, a peahen, a flock of small parrots, and other exotic, brightly colored tropical birds. (Neighborhood birds also like to stop by for a snack of peacock food.) Further to the rear, in the Ganesh Gardens, is a lovely koi pond well stocked with the requisite plump orange koi, as well as a sacred-to-Hindus peepal (bodhi) tree, a type of fig. Completing the complex are a number of overnight accommodations for travelers.

Opened in 1987, Govinda's is run by the Hare Krishna Hindu sect, whose ultimate aim (posted on a sign there) is to "respiritualize the entire human society."

Entering Govinda's walled compound, you'll find a relaxing patio where you can enjoy some excellent vegetarian or vegan food, as well as a koi pond, a small aviary (complete with peacock), and a number of overnight accommodations for travelers.

GOVINDA'S

WHAT A vegetarian restaurant and aviary

WHERE 711 E. Blacklidge Dr.

COST Lunch, $8.95; dinner, $10.95

PRO TIP Wednesdays and Thursdays are 100 percent vegan.

68

STATUE CONTROVERSY

Was Pancho Villa a hero or a murderer?

When it was unveiled at a public ceremony in 1981, the then-mayor of Tucson and a city councilman refused to attend. And it's remained a source of controversy in the decades since but has weathered every attempt to have it removed. The five-ton, fourteen-foot-high bronze statue of Mexican revolutionary Francisco (Pancho) Villa depicts the legendary general on horseback and was a gift to the city from the Mexican government and a Mexican journalists' association. It resides in leafy Veinte de Agosto Park, a one-acre green space in a prime location downtown where two main thoroughfares, Broadway Boulevard and Congress Street, split apart.

Depending on whom you ask, Villa was either a hero or a murderer. To many Mexicans and Mexican-American residents of Tucson, he was a champion of the oppressed and a hero of the 1910–1911 Mexican Revolution that deposed autocratic president Porfirio Díaz. (The government has given him a hero's burial in a crypt at the Monument to the Revolution in Mexico City.) Critics of the statue point to a Villa-led 1916

PANCHO VILLA STATUE

WHAT A controversial memorial

WHERE Intersection of W. Congress St., Broadway Blvd., and S. Church Ave.

COST Free

PRO TIP Due to recent park closures, you may have to view the statue from across the street.

The statue's Spanish-born sculptor, Julian Martinez, also created the statue of another historic figure, Father Eusebio Francisco Kino, which overlooks Tucson's South Kino Parkway.

A controversial statue of Mexican revolutionary Pancho Villa occupies a prime spot in downtown Tucson. To some, he's a hero; to others, a murderer who led deadly raids into U.S. territory more than a century ago.

massacre in the New Mexico border town of Columbus that left scores dead, as well as other raids and robberies along the border. U.S. General John "Black Jack" Pershing subsequently pursued Villa for months through northern Sonora, Mexico, to no avail. Villa was assassinated in 1923, but not before adding to his legend by playing himself in some early Hollywood movies.

A professor of Mexican-American studies at the University of Arizona recently summed up the only-in-Tucson nature of the controversy: "Each person who walks up to the statue has to ask questions about why [it] is here, right downtown," Lydia Otero told a local newspaper. "And they have to come up with their own answers. Why? Because we are Tucson, and it is complicated."

⁶⁹ HIGH FLYERS

Where can you "join the circus" in Tucson?

If your kids are threatening to run off and join the circus, don't panic—just head over to the Circus Academy of Tucson. Maybe your youngsters have dreamed about learning the art of acrobatics, or juggling, or stilt walking; Circus Academy will take them in and help them prepare for a life under the big top. Well, that may be a bit of a stretch, but several of their graduates have indeed gone on to careers teaching circus or operating their own circus schools. The academy's main goals, though, are to help any and all kids learn teamwork, increase their muscle and brain power, develop agility and a healthy body image—and have fun while doing it. Or maybe you still have dreams of developing circus skills as an adult. Circus Academy offers adult classes from rank beginner to advanced. (It generally takes about two and a half years to work your way up to the advanced levels.)

But aren't circus skills just for those with special talents? The folks at Circus Academy contend otherwise. Anyone, they say, regardless of body type, background, or ability level, can succeed at circus if they work hard and with focus. They maintain that academy performers start out with only a desire to learn and after sufficient training "seem to do the impossible." Circus skills taught there include aerial acrobatics (trapeze, silks); balance (tightrope walking, stilts, unicycle); props (juggling, spinning and balancing plates, twirling staves); and floor acrobatics (tumbling, handstands, contortion). The academy's director, Katherine Tesch, spent a decade as a circus performer herself after beginning her career in dance.

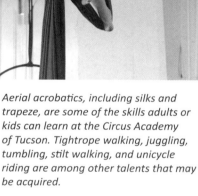

Aerial acrobatics, including silks and trapeze, are some of the skills adults or kids can learn at the Circus Academy of Tucson. Tightrope walking, juggling, tumbling, stilt walking, and unicycle riding are among other talents that may be acquired.

CIRCUS ACADEMY OF TUCSON

WHAT A place to learn circus skills

WHERE 400 W. Speedway Blvd.

COST Starts at $12 per class, but varies widely with program

PRO TIP A variety of instructional and intensive camps are available during the year.

The Circus Academy's professional troupe, Spider Silk Circus, is available for hire to entertain at special events—whether you need one performer or several.

70

A VINTAGE TRAILER COURT

Where can I stay in a 1955 aluminum Airstream?

Bisbee, Arizona, is just eleven miles north of the Mexican border, with a population of about 5,200. But it was once the biggest town between San Francisco and St. Louis and lies along old U.S. 80, a formerly well-traveled transcontinental roadway that once connected Savannah, Georgia, to San Diego. Today it's known for its rugged mountain atmosphere, copper mining history, specialty shops, art galleries, restaurants, and bars.

About an hour and a half's drive southeast from Tucson, Bisbee may be a good spot to stay overnight, especially when combined with a visit to the nearby Old West town of Tombstone. And that's where the Shady Dell Vintage Trailer Court comes in. It's a fixture along what is now State Route 80, and while it hasn't always been the Shady Dell, it's the site of Arizona's longest continuously operated trailer court.

The Shady Dell's memorable accommodations include eleven restored vintage trailers and a dry-docked Chris-Craft yacht, all manufactured between 1947 and 1959. Some of the stars of the lot are a 1955 aluminum Airstream, a 1951 Royal Mansion, a 1950 Hollywood Trailer, and a 1959 Boles Aero.

Needless to say, the theme here is 1950s to the max. Trailers are outfitted with a variety of throwback items like sock-hop-era phonographs and black-and-white TVs, and the décor—

Bisbee's Queen Mine Tour takes you deep into the now-closed mine that once produced a wealth of copper and other precious minerals.

The Old West mining town of Bisbee, just 11 miles north of Mexico, was once the biggest town between San Francisco and St. Louis. Now its streets are lined with shops and restaurants. The Shady Dell Vintage Trailer Court offers atmospheric retro lodging.

SHADY DELL VINTAGE TRAILER COURT

WHAT Retro lodging in Bisbee

WHERE 1 Old Douglas Rd., Bisbee

COST Accommodations $85 and up

PRO TIP Shady Dell closes some months in summer and winter; go to theshadydell.com to check availability.

individual to each trailer—runs to gold starburst walls, Polynesian tiki, porcelain swans, old *Life* magazines, Formica tabletops, and leopard-print carpets. Some have small kitchens with dishes and martini glasses recalling mid-century America, and each contains at least a small private toilet, with full bathroom and shower facilities nearby. The 1947 Chris-Craft, which isn't sailing anywhere soon, is decked out in vintage boat memorabilia.

71

POETIC EPITAPHS

Where are the bodies buried in Tombstone?

Along with whiskey and women, so the saying goes, life was cheap in 1880s Tombstone, known as one of the roughest boomtowns in the West. Consider the name of the town—Tombstone—and the name of the town's newspaper—*The Tombstone Epitaph*. The Bird Cage Theater (and brothel) counted more than two dozen dead among its patrons and 140 bullet holes in its walls during its heyday. Hangings, lynchings, shootings, stabbings, ambushes, and suicides were as common as poker cheats.

Which leads us to Boothill Graveyard, where cowboys were buried with their spurs on. Boothill, located just outside Tombstone, is the final resting place for most of the victims, along with other residents who died of natural causes—more than 250 in all. The sardonically poetic epitaphs engraved on some of its tombstones encapsulate the times.

Wells Fargo agent Lester Moore was shot during a dispute with a man over a package:

"Here lies Lester Moore,
Four slugs from a .44,
No Les, no more."

And pity poor George Johnson, who purchased a horse he didn't know was stolen:

"Here Lies George Johnson
Hanged by mistake 1882
He was right, we was wrong
But we strung him up, and now he's gone."

Tombstone, though—which prides itself as the "town too tough to die"—lives on as a tourist draw, not much more than an hour's drive from Tucson.

Boothill, just outside the Wild West boomtown of Tombstone, is the final resting place of many a local gunshot or hanging victim in the 1880s, when life was as cheap as whiskey. Perusing Boothill's tombstones, you'll find some colorful, poignant, and even amusing epitaphs.

BOOTHILL GIFT SHOP AND GRAVEYARD

WHAT A Wild West cemetery

WHERE 408 Arizona Hwy. 80, Tombstone

COST $3 per adult

PRO TIP Boothill is open daily 8 a.m. to 6 p.m.

Tombstone's famous Gunfight at the O.K. Corral, in which the Earp brothers and Doc Holliday killed three members of the Clanton Gang, lasted all of thirty seconds.

72

STAGE PRESENCE

How did the Invisible Theatre get its name?

First, let's be clear: Tucson's Invisible Theatre is not really invisible. But it is small and easily overlooked, occupying an eighty-seat theater in a residential neighborhood near the University of Arizona. And while it's been around long enough—nearly fifty years—to establish some name recognition, there remains the puzzling question as to what its intriguing name actually means.

INVISIBLE THEATRE

WHAT Creative theatrical productions

WHERE 1400 N. First Ave.

COST $30 (average ticket price)

PRO TIP The theater is closed during the summer months.

As the theater's artistic directors explain it, the Invisible Theatre derives its name "from the invisible energy that flows between a performer and audience, creating the magic of theater." It's been working such magic since 1971, when it offered a venue for local playwrights to showcase their work. And while it still performs that important function, it now also presents a broader range of productions ranging from classic dramas to recent Off-Broadway shows and musicals.

A recent example of the "invisible energy" came while staging the inventive *White Rabbit, Red Rabbit*, written by an Iranian playwright and performed by a single actor who was handed the script in a sealed envelope—the first time

Invisible Theatre productions also appear periodically in the 496-seat Berger Performing Arts Center at 1200 West Speedway Boulevard in Tucson.

While the Invisible Theatre is clearly visible, it can be easily overlooked in its quiet residential neighborhood. The name comes from "the invisible energy that flows between a performer and audience," according to its artistic directors.

he had ever seen it. With the help of audience participation and some creative written stage directions, the improvising actor managed to convey both humor and pathos as the playwright mused on the social interactions of experimental rabbits, the nature of life-and-death decision-making, and his own precarious situation as a writer in Iran. It's the type of cutting-edge theater that the Invisible Theatre offers in plain sight to those who wish to experience it.

73 STROLLING DOWN THE STRAVENUE

What the heck is a "Stra."?

It's generally easy to figure out which direction you're going in Tucson. For the most part, the roadways are laid out in a grid and are designated either avenues or streets, depending on their direction. If you're traveling on an avenue, it usually indicates you're taking a north-south route. If you're traveling on a street, you're most likely going either east or west. But what happens if the road cuts through part of the city on a diagonal?

That's when you get a "stravenue"—an only-in-Tucson portmanteau that puzzles many new arrivals and some Tucson old-timers as well. To qualify as a stravenue, a diagonal roadway must intersect both a street and an avenue. Tucson has about thirty such stravenues, marked on street signs by the abbreviations Stra. or Strav. (The official postal service designation for stravenue is Stra.) The first roadway to be so designated, the half-mile-long Cherrybell Stravenue, was named in 1949 and cuts southeast from Twenty-Second Street down to the central post office.

Since then, other stravenues have emerged, including Belford, Bryant, Camilla, Canada, Cerius, Concord, Desert, Dover, Drexel Manor, Fairland, Forgeus, Frankfort, Hartford, Helena, Hemlock, Holly, Howard, Kelvin, Lansing, Madison, McFee, Mendham, Menor, Miramonte, Nebraska, Olympia,

---

CHERRYBELL STRAVENUE

WHAT Tucson's first stravenue

WHERE Between E. 22nd St. and E. Silverbell Rd.

COST Free

PRO TIP The northeast corner of Cherrybell and 23rd Street offers a clear view of a "Strav" road sign.

In 1949, Cherrybell was named Tucson's first of some 30 stravenues—diagonal roadways that intersect both streets (which run east-west) and avenues (which run north-south). Watch for the abbreviated "Strav" on street signs throughout the city.

Ray, Rex, Tucson, and Venice. (In many cases, however, the stravenue designation is only applied to a portion of the roadway, so that you might find both South McFee Avenue and South McFee Stravenue conjoining each other.)

A number of stravenues were created in the wake of highway construction in parts of southeastern Tucson that chopped up city neighborhoods and disrupted the grid layout there. Several stravenues in the Pueblo Gardens neighborhood south of State Route 210 (Barraza-Aviation Highway) are a good example.

The stravenue moniker is said to have originated with the late local subdivision developer Roy Drachman, whose own name is now honored as a "Street"—not a "Stra."

⁷⁴ A GLIMPSE BACK IN TIME

What happened after the arrival of the "black robes"?

In the late seventeenth century, the "black robes," or Jesuit missionaries, arrived in what is now southern Arizona, carrying Christianity to the local Indian tribes. In 1691, Father Eusebio Francisco Kino founded a mission at Tumacácori, forty-five miles south of modern-day Tucson. It's far less visited than his later mission, the striking (and still active) San Xavier del Bac just south of the city. But the ruins of Tumacácori, now preserved in a National Historical Park, offer a riveting glimpse into a time when two disparate cultures—Spanish and Native American—both meshed and clashed.

For 130 more years, first under the Jesuits and later under the Franciscans, the Spanish brought new religion, language, agriculture, and protection from warring tribes to the Tohono O'odham people. But all too often they also brought cruelty, cultural destruction, and deadly diseases, such as smallpox and measles. The mission itself survived until 1848, twenty-seven years after Mexico's independence from Spain, when it was permanently abandoned and the residents moved northward to San Xavier del Bac.

On self-guided tours around the park, the mission church, built from 1800 to 1822 under the direction of Franciscans, still stands out despite its crumbling adobe brick walls and faded paint. On the outside, the facade, bell tower, and white dome remain attractive. On the inside, it bears little resemblance to the ornate, brightly painted church, replete with Baroque

---

Part of the Juan Bautista de Anza National Historic Trail extends from here to the town of Tubac, about two and a half miles north—and 1,200 miles farther to San Francisco.

One of the first missions established by Jesuit Father Eusebio Francisco Kino in the 1690s, the Tumacácori Mission south of Tucson is now a ruin that features the mission's adobe church, whose facade and bell tower remain well-preserved.

statuary, that it was two centuries ago, though scattered remnants of the initial décor remain.

Elsewhere in the park, there's a reconstructed O'odham *ki* (house) and an informative museum, as well as an orchard and garden with both indigenous and imported European fruit trees and plants, such as those that sustained hundreds of mission residents. The once-flowing nearby Santa Cruz River provided fish and water for irrigation.

TUMACÁCORI NATIONAL HISTORICAL PARK

WHAT Ruins of an early mission

WHERE 1891 E. Frontage Rd., Tumacácori

COST Adults, $7

PRO TIP On weekends, watch for outdoor demonstrations such as fresh tortilla making, ready for snacking.

A TOWN FILLED WITH FIRSTS

What was Arizona's earliest European settlement?

The small town of Tubac, about forty-five minutes' drive south of Tucson, is best known for its many art galleries, specialty shops, and restaurants, often swarmed with visitors. But it's much less known for its key role in the history of southern Arizona, best explored at Tubac Presidio State Historic Park. When Spanish soldiers established a presidio, or fort, in Tubac in 1752, it became the oldest European settlement in what is now Arizona, with a population of around five hundred by 1767. While that fort would close when the troops were moved to Tucson's new presidio in 1776, a second fort was established in Tubac eleven years later, and the town was continually occupied thereafter.

Tubac had several other "firsts" as well, including, fittingly enough, Arizona's first state park (Tubac Presidio), as well as Arizona's first newspaper printed on its first printing press. While Tubac's historic one-room schoolhouse is just the second-oldest surviving school in the state, it's one of the most interesting buildings to explore here. Note the blackboard instructions given to nineteenth-century teachers, advising that "women teachers who marry or engage in

In another Tubac "first," Arizona's first Spanish land grant was given to Don Toribio de Otero in 1789—on acreage now occupied by the Tubac Golf Resort & Spa.

A museum tracing the history of Tubac, which became Arizona's first European settlement in 1752, is a highlight of Tubac Presidio State Historic Park south of Tucson. The state park also features a historic one-room schoolhouse and an 1890s-era Sonoran row house.

other unseemly conduct will be dismissed" and "male teachers may take one evening each week for courting purposes." Boys and girls, meanwhile, risked getting ten lashes for playing cards or four lashes simply for playing anything together.

TUBAC PRESIDIO STATE HISTORIC PARK

WHAT Arizona's first European settlement

WHERE 1 Burruel St., Tubac

COST $7

PRO TIP The state park is located just beyond Tubac's main shopping area.

The only ruins left of the unwalled adobe presidio are on display behind glass, but you can amble through a desert garden and also view the rooms of an 1890s-era Sonoran-style row house, complete with outhouse.

Where can you find trendy shops in old shipping containers?

The Mercado San Agustín, which has been drawing crowds to its Spanish Colonial-style courtyard restaurants and shops since 1910, has recently been somewhat quietly joined by the MSA Annex, a short walk but a long distance in atmosphere away. Still a bit of a work in progress and almost overlooked in the midst of a West Side construction boom, the annex is a complex of rust-brown-colored shipping containers that have been transformed into a warren of locally owned small businesses and eateries.

Designed by Tucson architect Paul Weiner, the containers are modern, trendy—and snug—resulting in shops that are, for the most part, highly specialized, nicely curated, and upscale. Several eating places in the complex have more room to spread out, though, offering plenty of outdoor seating at reasonable prices.

The recently opened container complex has been steadily filling up with businesses, many owned by women or

MSA ANNEX

WHAT An unusual shopping area

WHERE 267 S. Avenida del Convento

COST Free to browse

PRO TIP The Mercado (down the street from the Annex) has a Thursday afternoon farmers market.

The Sun Link streetcar passes right by the MSA Annex near the western end of its route, making it convenient to reach from downtown or the University of Arizona campus.

The new MSA (Mercado San Augustin) Annex is a shopping complex constructed entirely from a series of used shipping containers. The snug containers house trendy clothing boutiques, shops featuring locally crafted furniture and home goods, a bicycle store, and restaurants with outdoor seating.

minorities. Dust and Heritage, which sells Sonoran Desert-inspired home goods; Why I Love Where I Live, stocked with Tucson-related items; and Mesa, which offers locally crafted small furniture, all have a decidedly homegrown flavor. Avenue Boutique features independently designed clothing, while Luca Ryann specializes in vintage wardrobes with a "modern twist." Dirt, promising "earthy vibes," peddles both potted cacti and incense.

For a change of pace or two, there's also Transit Cycle, a full-service bike shop, and Flam Chen, which creates "pyrotechnic" theater productions, something like a circus with fire elements. For sustenance and thirst, you can turn to Kukai Fresh Japanese Kitchen, Beaut Burger (note: it's all vegetarian), Hermosa Coffee, and Westbound, a bar and bottle shop.

INDIGENOUS GENIUS

Where can you find an outstanding collection of Native American craftsmanship and historical artifacts?

Even its staff members acknowledge that the Amerind Museum is off the beaten track. "Many people either haven't heard of it or they drive right past it," says one. Well, not exactly right past it. To reach the museum, you have to follow I-I0 about an hour east of Tucson (you know you're getting close when you start to see spectacular rock formations and multiple billboards hyping something called "The Thing"), take exit 318 (Dragoon Road), and, after a mile, turn onto a dirt road that leads to the museum complex just north of the little town of Dragoon.

Highlights include dazzling displays of Navajo, Zuni, Hopi, Apache, and Tohono O'odham artistry—exquisitely designed pottery and basketry, intricate beadwork, and ornate necklaces and bracelets of turquoise and silver—drawn primarily from northern Mexico and the American Southwest, an area inhabited for 13,000 years. Not to be missed are a Shoshone "story robe" painted on an elk hide and rows of children's dolls and cradleboards. (At any given time, curators display about 1,000 of some 35,000 objects in the collection.) Informative historical and archeological exhibits provide context. Next to the main museum, the Art Gallery presents special temporary exhibitions, often of Western art and photography.

While Amerind was founded as a research and archeological center in 1936 by Rose Hayden Fulton and William Shirley Fulton, who both died in the 1960s, the museum didn't open to the public until the 1980s—and is still awaiting the recognition it deserves.

Exhibits at the Amerind Museum include striking examples of Native American pottery and basketry often dating from the nineteenth century and before. Photos courtesy of Joe Kozlowski

AMERIND MUSEUM

WHAT A riveting look at Native American arts and culture

WHERE 2100 N. Amerind Rd., Dragoon

COST Adults, $12; seniors and students, $10; under 10, free

PRO TIP The Art Gallery closes between noon and 1 p.m. daily, so time your visit accordingly.

The museum offers a secluded picnic area framed by boulders and mesquite trees; there are no nearby restaurants.

78

WARTIME HYSTERIA

Where were some Japanese-Americans held during World War II?

During World War II, more than one hundred thousand Japanese-Americans, two-thirds of them U.S. citizens, were held in internment camps across the West. One of them was in Tucson, in what seems an unlikely spot for a prison: at an elevation of five thousand feet halfway up Mt. Lemmon, the highest peak in the Santa Catalina Mountains and a favorite outdoor getaway for Tucsonans. Just off the Catalina Highway leading up the mountain is the Gordon Hirabayashi Recreation site, named in honor of one of the internees, a then-college student who, after unsuccessfully challenging the constitutionality of President Franklin Roosevelt's 1942 detention order, served two ninety-day stints there. Today, the recreation site includes a campground and trailheads— along with the rocky ruins of what was then called the Catalina Federal Honor Camp. At various times the camp also housed

GORDON HIRABAYASHI RECREATION SITE

WHAT Japanese-American internment camp

WHERE Catalina Hwy., just past the Mile 7 marker.

COST $10 per vehicle for day use or camping

PRO TIP The campground is open November to April.

Using prison labor, the steep, winding twenty-seven-mile-long Catalina Highway was completed in 1951 and leads to additional campgrounds, hiking trails, a winter ski area, and the village of Summerhaven.

When President Franklin Roosevelt ordered Japanese-Americans to be held in internment camps during World War II, one was established halfway up Mt. Lemmon, where the prisoners helped build the Catalina Highway (pictured) that led up the mountainside. The site, now a recreational area, is named for one of the detainees.

bank robbers and embezzlers, as well as youthful offenders and a juvenile rehabilitation center, before shutting down in 1973.

The Japanese-Americans (most of whom were conscientious objectors moved from other relocation camps) were forced to work on the construction of the scenic Catalina Highway, which passes the very site where they were imprisoned. The Japanese internment camps were emptied after the war—a commission ruled that internees were victims of racial prejudice and wartime hysteria—and Hirabayashi's conviction was eventually overturned. The recreation site was renamed for him in 1999; he died in 2012 at age ninety-three.

79

TRACING LIVES

Why did Tucson's Jews almost lose their heritage?

Situated within Arizona's oldest synagogue—built in 1910, two years before statehood—Tucson's Jewish History Museum tells the story of the Jews who helped shape the city in perhaps surprising ways. As early as the 1850s, German Reformed Jews began migrating to Tucson in search of opportunity. They found it by becoming cowboys, ranchers, and merchants, with hopes of fitting in with the community. By 1883, the city had even elected its first Jewish mayor, Charles Strauss (there have now been five).

But as a museum docent points out, there was an ironic twist to their experience: "Even while they were influential in making Tucson more Jewish in values and learning," he says, "Tucson was actually making them less Jewish." For the most part, the early Jewish residents married Christians—and their religious heritage began to fade.

But a new wave of Jews arrived in Tucson following World War II, bringing their traditions with them. One of the most striking exhibits in the museum, "Mapping Migration: A Photographic Memoir Project", captures the lives of dozens of the city's Jewish families in three side-by-side images. The first was typically taken in the "old country," often in the early 1900s, before the families immigrated to the United States. The second group (usually including new generations) was taken in various preliminary stops in this country some decades later, while the third shows their progeny after moving to modern-day Tucson.

JEWISH HISTORY MUSEUM

WHAT Tucson's Jewish heritage exhibits

WHERE 564 S. Stone Ave.

COST Free

PRO TIP Open Friday 12 to 3 p.m., Saturday and Sunday 1 to 5 p.m.

Tucson's Jewish Heritage Museum, located within Arizona's first synagogue, tells the story of the city's Jewish community through docent-led tours and riveting audio and visual presentations. Next to the museum is the Holocaust History Center, focusing on genocides against Jews and other groups.

Next door to the museum is the attached Holocaust History Center, with exhibits not only on the genocide of the Jews in 1930s and 1940s Germany, but other more recent genocides around the world as well. It's a sobering reminder that we should all "Never forget."

Every other Friday from 11 a.m. to noon, the museum hosts talks on related topics of interest. Admission is free and comes with a bonus: two-for-one lunches at two nearby restaurants.

80

MORBID, YET STYLISH

What Tucson bar is set in an ex-mortuary chapel?

The Owls Club, a stylish cocktail bar that opened in late 2016, gives little indication of what's inside. Instead, it's marked by a sign for the historic Bring Funeral Home, the building's former occupant from 1928 to 2014. Extensive (and expensive) renovations by the new owners have done little to downplay its somewhat macabre setting—in fact, quite the opposite. They've set up the bar area in the ex-funeral parlor's chapel and created seating out of the onetime pews. The bar's slogan, "Let us live while we live," is a winking nod to its past as well. The lighting is kept very low, and the moody atmosphere is all the more heightened by dark wood, beamed ceilings, and stained glass windows.

Once your eyes have adjusted to the dark a bit it may be possible to read the drinks menu, which highlights six multi-ingredient house cocktails, a number of bottled and draught beers, a selection of Old World wines, and—the specialty here—nearly one hundred whiskeys: a variety of single malt scotches, bourbons, ryes, and more. The signature house cocktail, the Aspirational West, combines Irish whiskey with amontillado sherry, sweet vermouth, maraschino liqueur, and absinthe. The bartender will also fix up more standard drinks if you wish. Note that an additional room in back has couches for seating and is less noisy and less dim, though still moody.

The Owls Club takes its name from an 1880s-era social club run by well-to-do Tucson bachelors who hoped to meet prospective mates.

The Owls Club in downtown Tucson is a low-lit bar set in the chapel of a former mortuary, with seating on onetime pews and a deliberately moody atmosphere. Nearly 100 whiskeys are the specialty. If you find the sign that reads "Bring Funeral Home," you're in the right place.

OWLS CLUB

WHAT Ex-mortuary turned bar

WHERE 236 S. Scott Ave.

COST Drinks $2–$500

PRO TIP You'll find your smartphone's flashlight handy here.

81

ARTISTIC LICENSE

Where can you view your own artworks in a gallery?

If you've ever fantasized about having your artworks hanging in a bona fide gallery—or just want to see what a wide variety of Tucson artists are producing these days—welcome to the Solar Culture Gallery. Situated in a historic three-thousand-square-foot Art Deco former produce warehouse, the gallery shows the work of more than one hundred local artists and operates on a simple premise: bring in your artwork and they will display it, for free, no judgments given or questions asked. And if someone wants to buy your work, they don't take a commission.

So what's the catch? Well, nothing really, other than that you're limited to showing one big piece (four feet by four feet or larger) or up to three that are smaller. All sizes and mediums are acceptable. They do request that your work be ready to be hung on the wall—mounted with a strong, securely attached hanging device—unless it's a floor standing piece or sits on a base. You'll need to bring it in the week each show opens, one in October, one in February, and one in May, when they change all the art. That's it.

Solar Culture Gallery also presents live music events featuring national and international bands and other musicians with a decidedly New Age bent; ticket prices typically range from twenty to forty dollars and many are suitable for any age group.

SOLAR CULTURE GALLERY

WHAT Display your own artworks

WHERE 31 E. Toole Ave.

COST Gallery is free

PRO TIP Some of its musical events take place at other venues.

180

At the Solar Culture Gallery in Tucson's Warehouse Arts District, you can view your own artwork up on the walls, just by bringing it in – and it's free. The entrance to the gallery (pictured) is a distinctive work of art itself.

Solar Culture is located in the heart of Tucson's Warehouse Arts District, home to numerous artists' and photographers' studios and a big driver in revitalizing the downtown area.

82

A VOW WELL KEPT

Who sculpted those religious figures near the river?

Severely wounded in battle during World War I, sculptor Felix Lucero prayed to the Virgin Mary for survival. If his prayers were answered, he vowed to devote his life to creating Christian artworks. So goes the story behind the Garden of Gethsemane, a small public tract of religious statuary that resides in a gated garden across the Santa Cruz riverbed just west of downtown Tucson.

Lucero did live, but his life wasn't easy; by the late 1930s his home was a shack beneath Tucson's Congress Street Bridge. Still, he remained true to his vow, fashioning biblical statues from sand, silt, and debris that he gathered from the mostly dry Santa Cruz River, then covering the sculptures with gleaming white plaster. The centerpiece depicts Jesus with his twelve disciples at the Last Supper. Others display Christ on the cross, Jesus lying in his tomb, Pontius Pilate, and Joseph, Mary, and the baby Jesus.

Since Lucero's death in 1951, the statues themselves have somewhat miraculously survived the ravages of time and

GARDEN OF GETHSEMANE

WHAT Religious sculptures with a backstory

WHERE 670 W. Congress St.

COST Free

PRO TIP Parking is nearby in a lot just off West Congress Street.

The Garden of Gethsemane is easily accessed from Tucson's one-hundred-mile-long Loop Trail, which runs along the west side of the Santa Cruz River and attracts cyclists, walkers, and joggers.

At Tucson's Garden of Gethsemane, a gleaming white sculpture depicts the biblical Last Supper with Jesus and disciples. The garden's sculptures were fashioned by an indigent former World War I soldier who vowed to create such artworks if he survived his wounds.

vandalism. Most notably of late, the fingers of Jesus and several disciples have been missing, though volunteers have made various other repairs over the years. In the 1980s, the sculptures were moved to their current location near the bridge where Lucero once lived, now the underpass for the Congress Street exit along Interstate 10. The shaded sanctuary has since become popular as a wedding venue and as a retreat for prayer and reflection.

83 VILLAGE SQUARE AMBIANCE

What's the story behind Arizona's first shopping center?

It's now one of numerous little shopping areas along East Broadway Boulevard, but back when it was built in the mid-twentieth century, Broadway Village was Arizona's first commercial shopping center. In 1939, when it opened, much of the adjacent land was vacant. But its proximity to the upscale—and, at the time, suburban—neighborhoods of Colonia Solana and El Encanto Estates, as well as the Tucson Country Club and the luxury El Conquistador Hotel, was a key factor in its planning.

The developers, John and Helen Murphey, hired noted Swiss-born architect Josias Joesler to design the project, modeling it after a charming square in the Mexican village of Pátzcuaro that the Murpheys had encountered in their travels. The result was a splendid two-building Spanish Colonial Revival gem replete with clay tile roofs, red brick and burnt adobe surfaces, decorative ceramic tiles and ironwork, an arched breezeway, and carved niches.

BROADWAY VILLAGE

WHAT Arizona's first shopping center

WHERE Broadway Blvd. and Country Club Rd.

COST Free entry

PRO TIP Barrio Bread was a semifinalist for a 2019 James Beard Award.

Restaurants and other food purveyors dominate Broadway Village today, including Natural Grocers, Falora Pizza, Breakfast Club, Sushi Garden, and Barrio Bread.

Broadway Village, Arizona's first commercial shopping center, remains one of the most attractive. It was designed by noted architect Josias Joesler and modeled after a Mexican village square, complete with archway and flowers.

Joesler refined and expanded the original space until his death in 1956, when the prominent Mexican architect Juan Wørner Baz oversaw further expansion until its completion in 1961. While offering thirty-seven thousand square feet of retail space, the plaza retains its village square feel. It remains one of the most attractive developments along the busy Broadway corridor and has been awarded City Historic Landmark status.

The professional relationship between the Murpheys and Joesler continued. Over the course of three decades, they collaborated on more than four hundred buildings in Tucson, many with Spanish-style sensibility. As a result, Joesler—with the Murpheys' financial backing—is credited with helping to shape Tucson's national image as a romantic Southwestern destination.

84

URBAN TRANQUILITY

What makes a Japanese garden so different?

Just down the block from the heavily visited Tucson Botanical Gardens, the Yume Japanese Gardens are easily overlooked—but serenity is not often found in crowds. And finding serenity just off a busy Tucson street is what the Yume Gardens are all about. Opened in 2013, the Yume Gardens span three-quarters of an acre that inspire solitude and reflection.

Unlike a Western garden, a Japanese garden comprises both natural features and metaphorical elements—with stone and gravel, for instance, representing islands and the sea. At Yume, visitors will find five traditional visions of landscape: a stone and gravel garden, a courtyard garden, a Zen meditative garden, a dry river garden, and a strolling pond garden with koi pond. With shoes removed, you can also enter a replica of a typical cottage found in the Japanese countryside. It's like a little corner of Japan transplanted to the Sonoran desert.

Meaning "dream" in Japanese, Yume is the longtime dream of director Patricia Deridder. Belgian-born but a fifteen-year resident of Japan before moving to Tucson, Deridder's goal is to acquaint the city with the depth and richness of Japanese culture, enhanced by a museum displaying Japanese scrolls, kimonos, and other items and an art gallery that alternately features Japanese paintings, sculpture, photos, costumes, and ceramics. Yume offers classes in flower arranging, Japanese

---

YUME JAPANESE GARDENS

WHAT A tranquil Japanese garden

WHERE 2130 Alvernon Way

COST $13; ages 65+, $10; students, $9; ages 3–15, $6

PRO TIP Yume often closes following heavy rains or high heat; call 520-303-3945 to check status.

Yume Japanese Gardens imports a taste of traditional Japan to Tucson, with meditative gardens, koi pond, and other elements that provide a sense of tranquility. The gardens are also home to various festivals and special events throughout the year.

calligraphy, ink-brush painting, and origami, while tea ceremonies, Japanese music performances, and celebrations of seasonal festivals are on the docket of events. The gardens are open from October until early May.

Anyone suffering from grief or depression might benefit from Yume's Stroll for Well-Being program of guided therapeutic garden walks, which includes unlimited visits during the year ($260).

85

TAKE YOUR PICK

What's the first all-local food court in Tucson?

Tucked away amid a raft of Mexican restaurants, the American Eat Co., which opened in 2018, is Tucson's first food court featuring all-local eateries rather than national chains. Ensconced in a bright, airy space with industrial architecture and several types of seating, it offers diners ten different options for food and drink, making it ideal for families or people with divergent tastes. Several long tables in the center of the food court are designed to accommodate large parties, be they military from the nearby Air Force base, office workers having lunch together, or groups of friends out for a casual meal. Smaller tables and booths are found throughout, and a long row of counter seating is available as well.

Choices include Opa! Time for Greek food (gyros, salads); Dumb Fish—so named "because the smart fish never get caught"—for seafood, including poke; The Bite for sliders; the Arizona Rib House for barbecued ribs, wings, pulled pork, and sausages; Upper Crust Pizza for pizza by the slice; and Pinches for Mexican meals. You can also grab a coffee at Café Con Leche, indulge in some ice cream at Isabella's, or buy prime meats at a Mexican-style butcher shop. And there's a full bar with plenty of cushy seating nearby for a relaxing drink and conversation.

The butcher shop will cook you up a steak dinner on Friday and Saturday nights if you like.

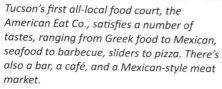

Tucson's first all-local food court, the American Eat Co., satisfies a number of tastes, ranging from Greek food to Mexican, seafood to barbecue, sliders to pizza. There's also a bar, a café, and a Mexican-style meat market.

AMERICAN EAT CO. & MARKET

WHAT An all-local food court

WHERE 1439 S. 4th Ave., South Tucson

COST Varies with purchase; inexpensive

PRO TIP Order your food at one of the counters and it will be brought to your table.

How can you find downtown's most historic sites?

The turquoise has faded in many locations and you might not even notice the thin greying stripe that runs along some sidewalks in downtown Tucson, but the Turquoise Trail is worth seeking out if you have an interest in the city's history. The trail—or at least a map of the trail—will guide you along a two-and-a-half-mile loop that leads past nearly two dozen of the city's most historic spots.

Created by the Tucson Presidio Trust for Historic Preservation, the trail begins, appropriately, at the Presidio San Agustín del Tucson Museum (196 North Court Avenue), a reconstruction of the site where Tucson was founded in 1775. You can pick up a map there to carry along with you (it's open Wednesday to Sunday, 10 a.m. to 4 p.m.) that identifies the historic sites. Maps are also available at the Tucson Visitor Center at 811 North Euclid Avenue near the University of Arizona campus.

THE TURQUOISE TRAIL

WHAT Two and a half centuries in two and a half miles

WHERE Start at 196 N. Court Ave.

COST Free (some historic sites along the route charge admission)

PRO TIP The map also shows other areas of interest you can see along the trail.

Some of the Turquoise Trail sites are quite well known, at least to most Tucsonans: Hotel Congress, the Fox Theatre, Old Town Artisans, and the Tucson Museum of Art and Historic Block. Other notable locations include the old Pima County Courthouse (which has just undergone an extensive renovation and is slated to hold the relocated University of Arizona gem and mineral museum), the Temple of Music and Art, and the Historic Railroad Depot. A

The turquoise itself may have faded in spots, but this trail along downtown Tucson's most historic sites is an excellent way to orient yourself to both well-known and more obscure spots. The trail begins at the Presidio Museum and continues for two and a half miles around the downtown area.

number of sites, though, are more obscure and easily overlooked, such as the Mormon Battalion Sculpture, the Garcés Footbridge and Gazebo, the Sosa-Carrillo Frémont House, La Pilita Patio, and Teatro Carmen.

Walking the loop straight through should take about an hour and a half, but you can easily break it up into segments and pick up where you left off another time.

Guided walking tours along the trail are offered at various times throughout the year; information is available at the Presidio Museum.

<u>87</u> ROCK STAR

Where can I find a good climbing gym in Tucson?

It's no secret that Tucson is hot in the summertime. So when rock climbers in most of the country are seeking out climbing opportunities during the warmer months, Tucson's climbers have to grapple not only with the next rock face or boulder but with temperatures that may hit 115 degrees. Cue Rocks and Ropes, a newly renovated and expanded indoor climbing gym that appeals to both veteran and aspiring climbers of all ages. High, colorful, 360-degree climbing walls include routes of varying difficulty that are continually changed to provide new challenges. Climbers can also tackle bouldering there, and it's all in air-conditioned comfort, with a friendly, helpful staff.

Of course, indoor climbing gyms can be useful throughout the year, including in Tucson, where it can get cold in the winters. Mostly they are safe, fun places for training and honing skills—requiring balance, strength, flexibility, and problem-solving—as well as for

ROCKS AND ROPES

WHAT An indoor rock climbing gym

WHERE 330 S. Toole Ave.

COST $18; under age 12, $12; equipment rental, $8

PRO TIP Hours vary throughout the year for members and non-members.

Both beginning and experienced climbers can get outdoors as well, via the Rocks and Ropes Outdoor Climbing School and Guide Service, which offers excursions to Mt. Lemmon and other locations.

Rocks and Ropes, a spacious, newly renovated indoor climbing gym, enables veteran climbers to practice their techniques during the heat of summer, as well as offering a safe facility for kids and newcomers to learn the sport.

introducing newcomers of any age to the sport. Children under twelve must first participate in one of their eight week-long summer camps (for ages five to fifteen) before they can take lessons at the gym. However, kids of any age can climb with a parent or other responsible adult and, on weekends, there are Kids Climbs for ages eleven and younger only, which come complete with belaying.

As with any endeavor that involves risk, climbers must first sign a liability waiver, and anyone under eighteen must have a parent or legal guardian sign. But equipped with harness, helmet, and the proper shoes (all available for rental if needed), climbers can set off with the assurance that safety is a high priority.

What's that little adobe doing on a busy downtown block?

It seems like an oddity now—a one-story Sonoran-style adobe hemmed in by far taller buildings on a busy block in downtown Tucson, and easy to overlook. The city's tallest structure, the UniSource Energy Tower, is nearby. But the historic Charles O. Brown House, one of the oldest standing dwellings in Tucson, was once a showplace owned by a prominent local family and features seventeen rooms arranged around a central courtyard. Against all odds, the house has somehow managed to survive for at least the last century and a half, even as downtown has experienced a building boom all around it. Its exact age is the subject of some dispute. While some of its roof beams have been determined to date from the 1840s, the builders may simply have used old wood during construction. More likely, alternate evidence shows, it dates from the 1870s, as do some of its other roof beams.

The house is named for Charles Owen Brown, a colorful nineteenth-century gun-toting character who owned the popular Congress Hall saloon and gambling hall, for which Congress Street is named. (The site of the saloon was the former home of the Territorial Legislature.) He and his wife, Clara, purchased the property in 1870, and they produced thirteen children before separating. Charles died in 1908, reportedly lost while searching for the legendary Iron Door

Because it was owned by the Arizona Historical Society and declared a historic landmark, the house survived destruction during Tucson's urban renewal projects of the 1960s and '70s.

The one-story adobe C. O. Brown House, one of Tucson's oldest standing dwellings, looks dwarfed between two modern downtown buildings, but in the 1870s it was a showplace owned by one of the city's most colorful early characters.

CHARLES O. BROWN HOUSE

WHAT One of Tucson's oldest surviving houses

WHERE 40 W. Broadway Blvd.

COST Free

PRO TIP Go inside the house to have a look at the surprisingly large central courtyard.

Mine in the Catalinas, said to be filled with gold. Clara remained in the house until 1932; it later became the Old Adobe Patio Restaurant and home to a variety of other businesses. It's now leased out for offices of several nonprofits, including the well-known local "Be Kind" promoters, Ben's Bells.

89 AN ARMORY LONG AGO

How did this peaceful neighborhood get its name?

Armory Park, Tucson's first residential neighborhood to be recognized on the National Register of Historic Places, has roots in the city's earliest days, when life in what was then

ARMORY PARK HISTORIC RESIDENTIAL DISTRICT

WHAT A neighborhood with a past

WHERE E. 12th St. south to E. 21st St. and Stone Ave. west to S. Jacobus Ave.

COST Free

PRO TIP If you have kids in tow, don't miss the Children's Museum at 200 South Sixth Avenue.

a small frontier village centered around the walled fort called El Presidio San Agustín del Tucson. Once known as Military Plaza, Armory Park housed both an armory and a contingent of soldiers who guarded the Presidio. Apparently the soldiers' rowdy behavior got out of hand, and eventually they were relocated to Fort Lowell on the outskirts of town, safely away from any residents. But the name Armory Park stuck.

Just south of downtown and within easy walking distance of the Historic Train Depot, Armory Park experienced its glory days after the arrival of the Southern Pacific Railroad in the 1880s. With the railroad carrying in needed building supplies such as brick, wood, and tin, railway honchos and other newly arrived eminences erected homes that forsook Mexican-style adobes in favor of more lavish styles imported from cities around the country. These included homes in the Victorian, Queen Anne, Territorial, and Greek Revival styles—characterized by a variety of wraparound porches, pyramidal roofs, turrets, and bay windows—that still dot the neighborhood's broad, tree-lined streets.

Tucson's historic Armory Park Neighborhood once housed an armory, then became a popular area for Southern Pacific executives to live after the railroad arrived in 1880. Homes with wrap-around porches, pyramidal roofs, turrets, and bay windows replaced traditional Sonoran styles.

The Armory Park Neighborhood also sports notable buildings such as the 1901 Carnegie Free Library (now the Children's Museum Tucson) and the 1915 Scottish Rite Cathedral. And, fittingly, it also harbors a grassy public square—also called Armory Park.

An adjacent development, Armory Park del Sol, built in 2000 on a site that housed railway workers, was reportedly the first planned solar-powered community in the country.

TUCSON'S FORGOTTEN SANATORIA

How did heliotherapy lead to a population boom?

A century ago, Tucson was one of the country's leading promoters of heliotherapy: the belief that the city's abundant sunshine, dry air, and warm climate could cure tuberculosis, then known as the "White Death" and rampant in the eastern United States. As early as the 1880s and '90s, local papers declared Tucson as the future chosen "sanatorium of the southwest" and labeled it the "health seekers' mecca and the invalid's paradise." According to a 1913 public health survey, half of Tucson's population—lungers, as they were called—had come here to seek cures for TB and other respiratory diseases.

By the mid-1950s, drug treatments had fostered a steep decline in TB rates, and most of the dozens of Tucson sanatoria that sprang up in the 1920s had closed down. A few were repurposed, however, and still stand today. Most notable is Veteran's Hospital No. 51,

SOUTHERN ARIZONA VA HEALTH CARE SYSTEM

WHAT A one-time TB sanatorium

WHERE 3601 S. 6th Ave.

COST Free

PRO TIP Since this is a working hospital, non-patient visits are restricted to the grounds.

For TB sufferers who flocked to Tucson seeking an elusive cure a century ago, the cruel irony was that the disease soon became Arizona's leading cause of death.

Today's VA hospital started life as a sanatorium treating tuberculosis patients, who flocked to Tucson from other parts of the country in the late nineteenth and early twentieth centuries in the wake of the TB epidemic known as the "white death."

opened in 1928 to treat some of the thousands of veterans who returned from World War I with TB. The imposing hospital, built on grounds of 116 acres south of downtown, was designed by Roy Place, a top local architect, and incorporated Spanish Colonial-style cloistered courtyards, fountains, and gold-domed towers.

Visitors are welcome to stroll the hospital's architecturally impressive "historic district," which spans about one-third of the overall grounds. The spacious facility was converted from a sanatorium to a general veterans' medical center in 1959.

SOURCES

1. **Gems, Minerals, and So Much More:** Personal site visit; Interview with Richard Ratkevich; http://www.tucsonmineral.com
2. **No Password, No Problem:** Personal site visit; https://www.reillypizza.com
3. **Going Batty:** Pima County Librarian Files, https:// www.library.pima.gov/contents/bats-in-Tucson; Watch Thousands of Bats Take Flight in Tucson, https://www.kgun9.com; Bats Under the Bridge: Who Knew?, https://www.southernarizonaguide.com; Mexican Free-tailed Bay Fact Sheet, https://www.desertmuseum.org/kids/bats
4. **Blooming Amazing:** https://www.tohonochul.org/bloom-watch; Stop What You're Doing! Queen of the Night is Blooming Tonight; https://www.tucson.com, July 18, 2017; Arizona-Sonora Desert Museum, A Natural History of the Sonoran Desert; Personal Site Visit
5. **Signs of Life:** Personal site visit; Interview with Monica Cook; https://www.ignitemuseum.com; Neon Sign Project/Tucson Historic Preservation Foundation, http://www.preservetucson.org/projects/neon-art-walk
6. **A Surprising Skirmish:** *History of Picacho Peak State Park* by Charles R. Eatherly; https://www.azstateparks.com/picacho/explore/park-history; https://www.azstateparks.com/picacho/camping-and-rvs/camping; https://www.southernarizonaguide.com/picacho-peak-civil-war-reenactment-slideshow; Personal site visit
7. **Holy Moai!:** Under a Giant Tiki Head on North Fourth Avenue, https://www.tucson.com, April 17, 2017; Tucson's Famous Giant Tiki Sculpture is Resurrected, by Jackie Stahl, *Arizona Foothills Magazine*, https://www.arizonafoothillsmagazine, 2017; Personal site visit
8. **Bear Down!:** The Story of Bear Down, Arizona Wildcats Sports official site https://arizonawildcats.com/sports/2013/4/18/208236191.aspx; Homecoming: Why Do Wildcats Bear Down? The Daily Wildcat, by Corrina Tellez, October 25, 2017; Why Do Arizona Wildcats Bear Down? https://www.azcentral.com, by Mark Nothaft, July 5, 2016; Bear Down Gym's Secrets, http://www.uofamystery.org/GhostsofBeardown.htm; Personal site visit
9. **The Lost Treasure of the Catalinas:** *The Search for the Lost Iron Door Mine of the Santa Catalinas* by Robert E. Zucker, http://www.azentertain.com/arizonagoldrush/lostmine; *The Escalante Mine is the Iron Door Mine* by Robert E. Zucker, http://www.azentertain.com/arizonagoldrush/lostmine/lostescalantemine.html; Relive the Legends of Arizona's Lost Treasure, by William Ascarza, *Arizona Daily Star*, October 12, 2014; Lost Mine with the Iron Door, by John D. Mitchell, *Desert Magazine*, July 1952
10. **An Enchanted Fantasyland:** https://www.tucsonvalleyofthemoon.com; Tucson Valley of the Moon, by Mark Nothaft, *Arizona Republic*, October 25, 2017; Atlas Obscura, Valley of the Moon, https://www.atlasobscura.com/places/valley-of-the-moon; Personal site visit
11. **Songs of Love and Sadness:** Mariachi Clothing and Popularity; How Did Mariachi Come to Be?; Mariachi: Not Just for Quinceañeras Anymore! https://www.mariachialegredetucsonaz.com; The History of the Tucson

International Mariachi Conference, by Gregory S. Rodriguez, https://www.tucsonmariachi.org, April 2018; Tucson International Mariachi Conference, https://www.visittucson.org/visit/events/mariachi-live; Tucson International Mariachi Conference, https://www.tucsonmariachi.org/espestacular-concert

12. **Bill Clinton's Fabulous Feast:** https:/www.minidito.com; Tucson in 100 Objects – the Menu at Mi Nidito, by Tom Beal, *Arizona Daily Star*, May 24, 2019; Personal site visit

13. **Mirror Images:** https://www.mirrorlab.arizona.edu; Atlas Obscura, https://www.atlasobscura.com/places/richard-f.-caris-mirror-laboratory; Personal site visit

14. **Toy Train Lovers' Dream:** http://www.gpdtoytrainmuseum.com; Personal site visit

15. **Hobnobbing with the Snobs:** Personal site visit; *Look Up, Tucson! A Walking Tour of Tucson*, Arizona, by Doug Gelbert, http://www.douggelbert.com/tucson-az; The Mansions of Main Avenue, https://explorationvacation.net/2014/06/historic-tucson-arizona-the-mansions-of-main-avenue/; History of El Presidio Inn, http://www.elpresidiobbinn.com; Snob Hollow, http://www2.lifeinusa.com/communities/tucson-az/snob-hollow-tucsons-historic-el-presidio

16. **Recycling for Parents:** http://www.littlebirdnestingco.com; Personal site visits

17. **That's No Mirage:** https://www.azgfd.com/fishing/community/tucson/kennedy; Urban Fishing: A Lot of People Are Hooked, by Scarlett McCourt, *Arizona Daily Star*, February 28, 2013; Urban Fishing Likely to Get City Approval, by Bud Foster, http://www.tucsonnewsnow.com, November 29, 2018; Personal site visit

18. **Arizona's First Commercial Vineyard:** https://www.sonoitavineyards.com; http://www.sonoitaelginchamber.org/winetasting.html; Personal site visit

19. **Welcome to Tucson:** Neon Saguaro Sign Harkens to Miracle Mile's Initial Glow, by Phil Villareal, Arizona Daily Star, April 6, 2010; 'Neon Pueblo' Lights Up Again as Tourist Draw, by Carol Ann Alaimo, Arizona Daily Star, January 18, 2012; Tucson, Arizona: 30-Foot-Tall Neon Cactus, https://www.roadsideamerica.com/tip/25254; Personal site visit

20. **John Dillinger's Bad Day:** Dillinger Gang Captured Here, by Fred Finney, Arizona Daily Star, January 26, 1934; Dillinger Captured in Tucson, www.library.pima.gov/blogs/post/dillinger-captured-in-tucson; Hotel Congress, Atlas Obscura, https://www.atlasobscura.com/places/hotel-congress; Personal Site Visit

21. **Monday Movement:** https://www.meetmeatmaynards.com; http://www.maynardsmarket.com; Personal site visits

22. **First Survive, Then Thrive:** http://www.tucsonchinese.org; Tucson in 100 Objects—Chinese Grocery, by Tom Beal, *Arizona Daily Star*, July 12, 2014; Personal site visit

23. **A Brilliant Bridge:** Luis G. Gutierrez-Cushing Street Bridge, www.

structuralgrace.com/luis-g-gutierrez-cushing-street-bridge; Solar Art, Zocalo Magazine, November 12, 2012; *What Few Have Seen: The New Luis G. Gutierrez Bridge Across the Santa Cruz* by Teya Vitu, Downtown Tucsonan, April 2, 2012; Our Story, July 30, 2018, https://www.facebook.com/luisggutierrezbridge; Personal site visits

24. **A Movie Star's Retreat:** Lee Marvin Lived, Worked, and Died in Tucson, by Elaine Raines, *Arizona Daily Star*, October 22, 2008; This Tucson Wow! House Used to Belong to Actor Lee Marvin, https://patch.com/arizona/tucson/tucson-wow-house-used-belong-actor-lee-marvin; Famed Actor Lee Marvin Fell in Love with Tucson, by Bill Norman, *The Desert Leaf*, September 2011; Personal site visit

25. **An Unlikely Transplant:** *Tucson Oddity: Hot Rod Shop's Lumberjack* by Brian J. Pedersen, Arizona Daily Star, June 8, 2009; Paul Bunyan, Legendary Character, https://www.britannica.com/topic/Paul-Bunyan; Muffler Man, https://www.roadsideamerica.com/tip/5876; https://www.celebrationpartyspot.com/tucsons-paul-bunyans-history.html; Personal site visits

26. **Ancient Agriculture:** Personal site visits; interview with Katya Peterson; http://www.tucsonsbirthplace.org; Mission Garden Will Take You Back Centuries, by Elena Acoba, *Arizona Daily Star*, May 7, 2016; Fruit Trees Re-Create Tucson's Birthplace, by Tom Beal, *Arizona Daily Star*, December 6, 2010

27. **Pharmaceutical Fantasia:** Personal site visit; interview with Stephen Hall; https://www.pharmacy.arizona.edu/centers/history-pharmacy/visitor-information; UA Museum Highlights Pharmacy History, by Savanah Modesitt, *The Daily Wildcat*, April 28, 2017

28. **Celebrity Locomotive:** http://www.TucsonHistoricDepot.org; Personal site visits

29. **Swap till You Drop:** http://www.tucsonswap.com; Personal site visit

30. **Desert Snow Play:** http://www.skithelemmon.com; Personal site visits

31. **The Mobster Next Door:** *'Joe Bananas' Both Loved and Hated in Retirement* by Arthur H. Rotstein, Associated Press, January 18, 1995; Joseph Bonnano, https://mafiafandom.com/wiki/Joseph_Bonnano; Joe Bonanno, http://www.doney.net/aroundaz/celebrity/bonanno_joe.htm; Bill Bonnano, Son of Famous Crime Boss, Dies in Tucson, *Tucson Citizen*, January 2, 2008; Mob Justice, by Jeff Smith, Tucson Weekly, July 22, 1999; Planned Parenthood Founder, Mafia Crime Boss, and Rodeo Called Tucson's Catalina Vista Home, by Jay Gonzales, *Arizona Daily Star*, November 28, 2016; Joseph Bonanno obituary, Associated Press, May 12, 2002; Joseph "Joey Bananas" Bonanno, https://www.findagrave.com/memorial/6454548/joseph-bonanno; Personal site visit

32. **Tucson's Past on Parade:** https://www.tucsonrodeoparade.com/the-museum; Interviews with personnel

33. **An Abundance of Aircraft:** "Boneyard"/AMARG Tour, https://www.pimaair.org/tour-boneyard; There's an Intriguing Airplane Boneyard in Arizona

That You Need to Visit, by Monica Spencer, https://www.onlyinyourstate. com/arizona/az-airplane-boneyard, December 14, 2016; Aircraft Boneyard Tour, https://www.roadsideamerica.com/story/64126; 309th Aerospace Maintenance and Regeneration Group, Atlas Obscura; Personal Site Visit

34. **Backstage at a Movie Palace:** Personal site visit; interview with Tom Skinner; https://www.foxtucson.com

35. **Secluded Setting:** *Colonia Solana—One of Tucson's Historic Residential Districts* by Nick Labriola, https://www.realtucson.com, July 29, 2014; Historical Tucson by William C. Barrow, *The Saguaro*, June 1986; Colonia Solana Residential Historic District, https://www.livingplaces.com; *A Guide to Tucson's Historic Neighborhoods* from the Blenman-Elm Neighborhood Association; Personal site visits

36. **A Classy Classic Neighborhood:** El Encanto: An Enchanting Place to Get Lost, by William C. Barrow, *The Saguaro*, August 1986; *El Encanto Estates—A Beautiful Historic Neighborhood in Midtown Tucson* by Nick Labriola, https://www.realtucson.com, May 7, 2015; Street Smarts: Contest Named Streets of El Encanto Estates, by David Leighton, *Arizona Daily Star*, September 1, 2014; *A Guide to Tucson's Historic Neighborhoods* from the Blenman-Elm Neighborhood Association; Personal site visits

37. **A Chicano Music Legend:** http://www.laloguerrero.com; Sense of Humor Earns Fame, Fortune for Guerrero, by Pat Moran Benton, *Arizona Daily Star,* October 6, 1978; Guerrero Dies: Hero to Latin Musicians, by Gerald M. Gay, *Arizona Daily Star*, March 18, 2005; Personal site visit

38. **Farcical Follies:** Interview with David Hoffman, producer; Personal site visit

39. **History on Horseback:** www.ranchodelaosa.com; Interview with ranch personnel

40. **Movable Art:** https://www.matbevelcompany.org; Kiwanis Learns About Beveldom, The Alliance Review, August 11, 2017; Kinetic Saturdays Make Art Sing at Mat Bevel, by Breagh Watson, *The Daily Wildcat*, April 3, 2017; Man Behind Bevel, Scientist Among Artists, By Leah Gilchrist, *The Daily Wildcat*, March 29, 2017; Mat Bevel's Museum of Kinetic Art Puts a Spin on Modern Day Art, By Victoria Hudson, *The Daily Wildcat*, November 5, 2016; Atlas Obscura, https://www.atlasobscura.com/places/mat-bevels-museum-of-kinetic-art; Ark D'Bevel Docks: Sets to Disembark., by Jamie Manser, *Zocalo Magazine*, July 1, 2014

41. **Faded Glory:** Can Tucson, Arizona, Bring Back its Miracle Mile? by Gideon Berger, *Cities Speak*, March 23, 2018; Restoring Miracle Mile, by Laura Markowitz, https://www.azpm.org, August 4, 2011; Miracle Mile Recognized on National Register of Historic Places, https://www.azpm.org; Personal site visits

42. **Vintage Car Showcase:** http://www.franklinmuseum.org; The Franklin Auto Museum in Tucson, http://www.classiccartravelguide.com; Personal site visit; interview with museum guide

43. ***Carne, Por Favor:*** Personal site visits

44. **Speed Demons:** https://www.autobahnspeed.com; Personal site visit
45. **Last of a Breed:** http://www.casavideo.com; http://www.casafilmbar.com; Personal site visits; interviews with personnel
46. **A City within a City:** https://www.southtucsonaz.gov; South Tucson Looks to Double its Square-Mile Size, by Luis F. Carrasco, *Arizona Daily Star*, May 26, 2015; Tax Fears Formed S. Tucson, Now Famous for its Food, *Arizona Daily Star*, December 14, 2010; Personal site visits
47. **Lyrical Mystery:** McCartney Ranch Was Linda's Favorite Spot, *Deseret News*, April 25, 1998; The Beatles' Ties to Arizona Go Deeper Than "Get Back," by Mark Nothaft, Arizona Republic, January 4, 2018; Paul McCartney's Arizona Ranch, by Dennis Begin, *RV West*; It was 50 Years Ago: the Beatles and Tucson, by Cathalena E. Burch, *Arizona Daily Star*, May 8, 2018; "Get Back"—Tucson, Arizona, https://www.songfacts.com/place/tucson-arizona/get-back; Personal site visit
48. **Pearl Harbor Pathway:** UA's Mall Memorial Makes "Quiet Statement," by La Monica Everett-Haynes, UA News, December 5, 2016; http://www.ussarizonamallmemorial.org; Personal site visits
49. **A Christmastime Treat:** https://www.tucsonmuseumofart.org/la-casa-cordova; This Elaborate Tucson Nativity Fills an Entire Room and Will Blow Your Mind, by Ann Brown, *Arizona Daily Star*, December 4, 2017; This Nativity Scene is an 800-Piece Marvel, by Ann Brown, *Arizona Daily Star*, November 7, 2014; Personal site visit
50. **A Living Laboratory:** https://www.tumamoc.arizona.edu; App Gives New Perspective to Walk Up Tumamoc Hill, by Stacy Pigott, University of Arizona, September 2017; Everything You Need to Know Before You Hike Tumamoc Hill, https:www.tucsontopia.com/tumamoc-hill; Personal site visits
51. **Unsung Landmark:** Tucson Oddity: Old Water Tower Now Historical Landmark, by Andrea Rivera, *Arizona Daily Star*, December 6, 2010; Historic Tower Now a Landmark, by Peter Pegnam, *Tucson Citizen*, May 4, 1994; El Conquistador Revisited, by Rock Wiley, *Arizona Daily Star*, August 21, 2011; Personal site visit
52. **Going Peacefully Postal:** https://www.postalhistoryfoundation.org; Personal site visit
53. **Lost Barrio Find:** http://www.romaimports.com; Personal site visits
54. **Not Your Average Selfie:** https://www.ccp.arizona.edu; Personal site visit
55. **The Games People Played:** Hohokam Ballcourt World, Archaeology Southwest, January 2018; *The Mystery of Hohokam Ballcourts* by Alexandra Witze, https://www.archaeologicalconservancy.org, March 15, 2018; Hike into History on the Romero Ruin Trail North of Tucson, by Doug Kreutz, *Arizona Daily Star*, March 28, 2018; Romero Ruin Interpretive Trail: Tracing Human History in the Area, by Doug Kreutz, *Arizona Daily Star*, February 11, 2007; The Hohokam, by D. Rose, http://www.arizonaruins.com/articles/hohokam/hohokam.html, February 2014; https://www.azstateparks.com/parks/catalina; Personal site visit

56. **Birding Bonanza:** Sweetwater Wetlands, www.tucsonaudobon.org/go-birding; Sweetwater Wetlands, www.tucsonaz.gov/water/sweetwater-wetlands; Tucson Bird Watching, www.visittucson.org/things-to-do/day-trips/birding-watching; Personal site visit

57. **A Futuristic Flop:** www.biosphere2.org; The Lost History of One of the World's Strangest Science Experiments, by Carl Zimmer, *New York Times*, March 29, 2019; Tales from the Morgue: Locked in at Biosphere 2, by Johanna Eubank, *Arizona Daily Star*, September 25, 2018

58. **Playing Pioneer:** www.tucsonpresidio.com/visit; Personal site visit

59. **Colossal Hideout:** https://www.colossalcave.com/bandits; Colossal Cave, https://www.desertusa.com/desert-arizona/colossal-cave.html; Colossal Cave, Atlas Obscura

60. **Celebrity Rehab:** https://www.sierratucson.com; http://www.doney.net/aroundaz/celebrity/douglas_michael.htm; http://www.doney.net/aroundaz/celebrity/downeyjr_robert.htm; http://www.doney.net/aroundaz/celebrity/celebrity_l.htm; http://www.doney.net/aroundaz/celebrity/celebrity_s.htm; Third Sierra Tucson Patient Death in 13 Months, by Stephanie Innes, *Arizona Daily Star*, February 7, 2015; http://www.cottonwooddetucson.com

61. **In Search of Crested Saguaros:** https://www.nps.gov/sagu/learn/nature/why_crested.htm; *Crested Saguaro—Mystery of the Arizona Desert* by Andrew Brown, Arizona Public Media, May 22, 2016; The "Crest Quest" has found 2,237 Rare Crested Saguaros around Tucson, Elsewhere, by Doug Kreutz, *Arizona Daily Star*, October 1, 2018; Q&A: The Rare Crested Saguaro, *Arizona Highways*, March 21, 2017; 8 Things You Might Not Know About the Saguaro Cactus, by S.E. Schlosser, the *Arizona Republic*, August 4, 2015; Personal site visit

62. **Snaking Around:** Rattlesnake Bridge, by Dean Jeffrey, https://www.roadsideamerica.com/story/15070, July 21, 2002; Diamondback Bridge, https://www.atlasobscura.com/places/diamondback-bridge; Rattlesnake Bridge, https://www.visittucson.org/business/rattlesnake-bridge; Basket Bridge Dedication Set, by Greg Bryan, Arizona Daily Star, Nov. 15, 2007

63. **The Wishing Shrine:** Big Jim: Some History About El Tiradito, by Jim Griffith, *Arizona Daily Star*, May 21, 2013; Historic American Landscapes Survey—El Tiradito, https://www.tucsonaz.gov/files/preservation/ElTiradito_HALS_AZ-8.pdf; El Tiradito National Register of Historic Places Inventory—Nomination Form, by James Garrison from Arizona State Historic Preservation Office, 1975; El Tiradito, *Visit Tucson*, https://www.visittucson.org/seven-beaten-path-choices-savvy-visitor; Barrio Viejo—History, www.barrioviejo.com/history.html; Tucson, Arizona: Wishing Shrine of El Tiradito, by Kaitlyn Barrett, https://www.roadsideamerica.com/tip/28802, May 4, 2011

64. **A Quirky Royal Manse:** Personal site visit interview with owner Daniel Reese

65. **Seeds of Life:** Personal site visits; https://www.native seeds.org

66. **A Slice of the Midwest:** http://www.winterhavenfestival.org; https://www.winterhavenrides.com; Neighborhood Spotlight: Winterhaven, by Nick Labriola, https://www.realtucson.com/2010/06/19/neighborhood-spotlight-winterhaven, June 19, 2010; Personal site visit

67. **A Walled Oasis:** https://www.govindasoftucson.com; Eat Your Way to Spirituality at Govinda's Natural Food Buffet, by Craig S. Baker, *Tucson Foodie*, January 17, 2018' Personal site visit

68. **Statue Controversy:** Pancho Villa Statue Unveiled in Arizona, *New York Times* archive, July 2, 1981; Tucson's Pancho Villa Statue Survives Another Push to be Removed, by Curt Prendergast, *Arizona Daily Star*, December 18, 2018; Tucson Won't Remove Pancho Villa Statue, Despite Conservative Group's Request, Associated Press, December 17, 2018; Infamous Tucson Statue Pancho Villa Will Stand After Group Tries to Have it Removed, by Claudia Kelly-Bazan, KGUN9, December 12, 2018; Tucson, Arizona: Pancho Villa, U.S. Invader, https://www.roadsideamerica.com/tip/51657, April 6, 2016

69. **High Flyers:** https://www.circusacademytucson.com; Personal site visit

70. **A Vintage Trailer Court:** http://www.theshadydell.com; Trailer-Cachet: Luxury Vintage Airstreams Are Turned into Trendy Hotel Rooms at Retro 1950s-Themed Court, by Mollie Cahillane, https://www.DailyMail.com, September 4, 2017; The Shady Dell, by Kelly Vaughn, *Arizona Highways*, https://www.arizonahighways.com/eat-sleep/lodging/shady-dell; Vintage Trailer Court Takes Tourists Back in Time, by Matt York, Associated Press, September 4, 2017; The Retro Bliss of Vintage Trailer Resorts, by Erin E. Williams, *The Washington Post*, March 8, 2019; Personal site visit

71. **Poetic Epitaphs:** Boothill Grave Yard—A Descriptive List of More Than 250 Graves in Boothill; Head to Tombstone, Arizona for an Offbeat Western Adventure, by Andi Berlin and Samantha Munsey, www.tucson.com, March 20, 2018; Personal site visit

72. **Stage Presence:** http://www.invisibletheatre.com; Personal site visit

73. **Strolling Down the Stravenue:** Road Runner: "Stravenue": Is It Unique to Tucson?, by Andrea Kelly, Arizona Daily Star, March 3, 2008: Cherrybell Stravenue, Atlas Obscura, https://www.atlasobscura.com/places/cherrybell-stravenue: Personal site visit

74. **A Glimpse Back in Time:** https://www.nps.gov/tuma; This Road Trip to Tumacácori is the Perfect Quick Holiday Adventure, by Andi Berlin and Samantha Munsey, www.tucson.com, November 28, 2018; Personal site visit

75. **A Town Filled With Firsts:** https://www.azstateparks.com/tubac; Personal site visit

76. **Container Chic:** https://www.mercadodistrict.com/annex; Personal site visit

77. **Indigenous Genius:** Personal Site Visit

78. **Wartime Hysteria:** Dark Side of U.S. History That Built Catalina Highway, by Tobey Schmidt, *Arizona Sonora News*, February 23, 2017; Prison Camp

Once a Part of Tucson, by Albert Vetere Lannon, *Desert Times*, December 2, 2015; Onetime Internment Camp in Catalina Mountains Offers Lesson in History, by Doug Kreutz, *Arizona Daily Star*, December 27, 2016; Gordon Hirabayashi Campground, Coronado National Forest, www.fs.usda.gov/recarea/coronado/recarea/?recid=25648; Personal site visit

79. **Tracing Lives:** https://www.jewishhistorymuseum.org; Personal site visit
80. **Morbid Yet Stylish:** Historic Bar Revived Inside Former Funeral Home, by Lauren Eads, httos://www.thedrinksbusiness.com, October 18, 2016; Is Owls Club Haunted? By Ivy Morris, Arizona Travels, December 6, 2016; Here's What to Drink at Downtown Tucson's Newest Bar, Owls Club, by Andi Berlin, www.tucson.com, November 30, 2016; Personal site visit
81. **Artistic License:** http://www.solarculture.org; Personal site visit
82. **A Vow Well Kept:** Garden of Gethsemane, https://www.roadsideamerica.com/story/15069; Garden of Gethsemane, https://www.atlasobscura.com/places/garden-of-gethsemane; Personal site visit
83. **Village Square Ambiance:** http://www.broadwayvillagetucson.com; Broadway Village, by Poster Frost Mirto, *Architecture/Planning/Preservation*, August 2015; Joesler and Murphey, an Architectural Legacy for Tucson, University of Arizona, 2000; Personal site visit
84. **Urban Tranquility:** http://www.yumegardens.org; Personal site visit
85. **Take Your Pick:** https://www.americaneatco.com; Personal site visits
86. **Semi-Turquoise Trail:** Turquoise Trail, https://www.tucsonpresidio.com/turquoise-trail; Personal site visit
87. **Rock Star:** https://www.rocksandropes.com; Personal site visit
88. **A Historic Oddity:** Results of Archaeological Monitoring and Data Recovery at the Charles Owen Brown House, https://www.tucsonaz.gov/files/preservation/Brown_House.pdf; Under the Floors: Archaeology Inside the Brown House, *Desert Archaeology*, August 24, 2018; Personal site visit
89. **An Armory Long Ago:** Armory Park, https://www.visittucson.org; Tucson's First Historic Neighborhood, http://www.planetlinks.com/armoryparkdelsol/community/armoryparkhistory.html; Downtown Living at its Best, by Nick Fabriola, https://www.realtucson.com, May 5, 2014; Personal site visit
90. **Tucson's Forgotten Sanatoria:** The White Plague in Tucson, Arizona, 1880-1945, National Register of Historic Places; Sanatoria Architecture in Tucson, Arizona, 1880-1945, National Register of Historic Places; Southern Arizona VA Health Care System, https://www.tucson.va.gov/about/history.asp; Personal site visit

INDEX

Photo courtesy of Pixabay.